Understanding Your Grief

Also by Alan Wolfelt

Healing the Bereaved Child:
Grief Gardening, Growth Through Grief
and Other Touchstones for Caregivers

Healing Your Grieving Heart:
100 Practical Ideas

Healing A Friend's Grieving Heart:
100 Practical Ideas for Helping
Someone You Love Through Loss

Healing a Parent's Grieving Heart:
100 Practical Ideas After Your Child Dies

The Journey Through Grief:
Reflections On Healing

Companion
P R E S S

Companion Press is dedicated to the education and support of both the
bereaved and bereavement caregivers. We believe that those who
companion the bereaved by walking with them as they journey in grief
have a wondrous opportunity: to help others embrace and grow
through grief—and to lead fuller, more deeply-lived lives themselves
because of this important ministry.

For a complete catalog and ordering information,
write or call:

Companion Press
The Center for Loss and Life Transition
3735 Broken Bow Road
Fort Collins, CO 80526
(970) 226-6050
www.centerforloss.com

Understanding Your Grief

Ten Essential Touchstones for Finding Hope and Healing Your Heart

Alan D. Wolfelt, Ph.D.

Companion
PRESS

Fort Collins, Colorado
An imprint of the Center for Loss and Life Transition

Companion Press is an imprint of the
Center for Loss and Life Transition,
3735 Broken Bow Road, Fort Collins, Colorado 80526.

Printed in the United States of America

12 11 10 09 08 07 06 05 04 03   5 4 3 2 1

ISBN: 1-879651-35-1

To the thousands of journeyers who have invited me to walk with them through the wilderness of their grief. What you have taught me I teach to others. Thank you for entrusting me with your stories.

Contents

Foreword

by John DeBerry

Sitting on a table, legs swinging back and forth, shirtsleeves rolled up. This was Alan Wolfelt the first time I met him.

I was attending a class he was teaching on understanding and supporting grieving families. As he shared his viewpoints and experiences, I saw that his posture matched his teaching style—relaxed and genuine. He was speaking from his heart.

Soon after, I participated in Alan's grief support group facilitator training. At week's end he gave each of us a copy of *Understanding Grief: Helping Yourself Heal*—the precursor to the book in your hands. I read it promptly and loved it. From the spring of 1996 through the fall of 2003, we used *Understanding Grief* as the basis for 40 support groups at Chicago's Northwestern Memorial Hospital's hospice program. The response was uniformly positive. "Where can I get more copies of this book?" was a common comment. Another woman said exuberantly, "It made me feel so validated!" And so it's been for eight years.

And now we are the fortunate recipients of Dr. Wolfelt's new text, *Understanding Your Grief*. What greater impact can a teacher have than to provide students with tools to facilitate their learning! Those of us who know his work—his teaching, his speaking, his writing—take for granted that it will be replete with helpful, informative counsel. This book is no exception.

Understanding Your Grief contains all the truly useful information and compassionate guidance that *Understanding Grief* did and more. I urge you to read both the Preface and the Introduction, for they are an important prelude to what follows. While words may seem feeble at this time, allow Dr. Wolfelt to mentor you on your journey. In your own time, and at your own pace, and in your own way, be an active participant as you set your intention to heal and begin reconciling your loss. Surrender to the process.

This book addresses a multitude of questions that I, and other grief counselors, are often asked. "Am I going crazy?" "Am I the only one who feels like this?" "Why doesn't anyone else seem to be acting/feeling this way?" In his reader-friendly, non-prescriptive way, Alan shares information on the various dimensions of grief that may be experienced. Yet he also emphasizes that each mourner's journey is unique, and that while there may be similarities, there will also be differences.

"He who has no time to mourn has no time to heal," wrote poet John Donne. When you feel ready to embrace your changed heart, know that the Touchstones await you on your journey through uncharted territory. As you walk the path, pause and reflect on memories of the person you loved. Remembering may be painful. It can also be heartwarming. Tenderly cradle your thoughts and feelings. Take time to express them.

The companion *Understanding Your Grief Journal* will help you with this expression, with this process of "getting what's on the inside out." As Alan teaches, it is in mourning that we heal. Journaling, along with tears and talking, can clarify aspects of the journey and enhance your healing.

In the end is the beginning... "I give back what I learn," Alan once told me. Indeed, in this book Alan gives back what he has learned. Now it is your turn to learn and, in time, to give back to others. Read *Understanding Your Grief* slowly and gently. Many gifts await you. Peace and blessings for a most successful healing journey.

John DeBerry, M.A., M.P.S., C.T.
Bereavement Coordinator, The Palliative Care and Home Hospice Program
Northwestern Memorial Hospital, Chicago, Illinois

October, 2003

Preface

In 1992 I wrote a book entitled *Understanding Grief: Helping Yourself Heal*. In it, I sought to affirm each mourner's unique thoughts and feelings while normalizing common grief responses. I have been honored to find that thousands of people discovered hope in their healing through using this resource.

Here it is more than a decade later. Over these years, I've continued to learn from the people who allow me to sit with and "companion" them in their grief. I have changed and, I like to think, grown, both as a caregiver and as a human being. I can only hope that the following pages reflect some newfound maturity and wisdom. (If not, at least I know I now have some gray hair!)

It was only natural that as I reached my forties I would come to experience more personal losses in my own life. I committed myself years ago to honoring other people's stories—stories of love and loss, pain and joy, hopes fulfilled and dreams lost. I have a passion for helping people. But almost four years ago I needed help myself. My wonderful, loving father died at 72 of malignant melanoma. My gift and my grace was that I had, and continue to have, friends and family who have supported me in my need to openly and honestly mourn my father's death.

Before my father died, it was my privilege to honor his life story. Toward the end, my wonderful father recognized in his head and heart that his days on this earth were limited. Rest did not come easy, but his need to "story" did.

His love of family flowed out of stories from his childhood. He told me how his mother inspired his love for baseball. He told me how his father wasn't very emotionally or physically available to him as he grew from childhood to adolescence. He told me of his deep love for his older brothers and sisters.

In the midst of my awareness that I would soon not have my father in my life, I listened and I learned. I affirmed that his love for me was true and abiding. I learned of his fears about my mother, who survives him. I learned what I already knew—my father was a great man, a loving husband, and a wonderful father.

I also learned about the awesome power of "telling the story." As he shifted from topic to topic, he didn't need me to get in the way. As he at times struggled with a specific detail of a long-ago memory, he didn't need me to get in the way. As he was brought to tears by his love-filled memories of life and living, he didn't need me to get in the way.

Honoring my father's story also blessed me with a sacred moment. As I was helping him prepare to leave the hospital, he gave me a "high five," and with a glint in his eye he said, "Thanks for listening. Thanks for helping me make a plan to go home." Oh, yes, the awesome power of the story.

Thanks, Dad, for reminding me not only of your love for me and our family, but of how all of us need to stop—to listen— and to honor stories about life and death. Thanks for making me proud to be a grief counselor and companion to my fellow human beings. But most of all, thanks for making me proud to be your son.

The death of my father and the opportunity to be a grief teacher and healer have continued to enrich my life, my living, and my loving since the first version of *Understanding Grief*. These experiences have also continued to "teach me" about the mystery of grief and mourning. In the following pages, I discuss what I have learned in the past decade and offer it up to you, the reader. Perhaps you can think of this book and its contents as an invitation—an invitation to tell your story of grief and healing!

Acknowledgments

I owe a debt of gratitude to many people who inspired the creation of this book and made possible its production.

I must first thank my early mentor Ken Dimick, who first encouraged me to share myself with the world through my writings and teachings. I am appreciative of Ken, not only for urging me to write down my thoughts, but also for his enthusiasm for my efforts to help people mourn life losses.

Another early mentor was Virginia Satir, who has since died. She was the first person to help me understand that the healthiest member of the family in grief is usually the "identified patient."

John DeBerry has been a true friend and long-time supporter of my life's work. He has facilitated dozens of support groups using my books as a foundation for his helping efforts. When I turned my thoughts to who might best introduce this new book through a Foreword, I immediately thought of John. His words invite readers to open their hearts and enter into the journey that is *Understanding Your Grief*.

Karla Oceanak has been my editor since 1992. I thank her for her insight and commitment to this book. Someone once told me that an editor is a friend who keeps you from looking foolish. Karla has been this kind of friend. For that and for her belief in my ability to write, I thank her with all my heart.

My friend and co-author of another of my books, Raelynn Maloney, was kind enough to offer to review this manuscript and suggest subtle, yet critical, improvements. I thank her for her enthusiasm, her sensitivity to the needs of those in grief, and her authentic friendship.

My graphic artist, Angela Phillips-Hollingsworth, checked and rechecked the accuracy of this book's design, even through multiple rounds of changes. I appreciate her "can-do" attitude!

My assistants, Makiko Parsons and Kathy Anderson, helped keep me grounded during the natural chaos that comes with writing a book while meeting all the demands of running the Center for Loss and Life Transition. Thank you, Maki and Kathy!

A book is nothing without an audience. I would like to acknowledge my book distributor, Independent Publishers Group, who helps me get this resource into the hands of those who will draw on it to find hope for healing.

My friend Kirby Duvall accompanied me on my hike in Aspen, Colorado,when I took the photographs for this book. I thank him for his friendship.

In my thirty years as a grief counselor and educator, I have had the privilege to meet and "walk with" thousands of mourners. They have shared their grief journeys and intimate lives with me. Without them this book would not be, nor would I be who I am.

And I could never forget my family, who makes all things possible.

Introduction

"The clearest way into the Universe is through a forest wilderness."
John Muir

Understanding As Surrendering

The title of this book is *Understanding Your Grief*. Indeed, one of the most important things I do in my ministry to grieving people is provide information that helps them (and you!) integrate loss into their lives. What's more, I strive to help them understand and avoid some of the unnecessary pain sometimes caused by well-intentioned but misinformed friends, family members, and even some professional counselors. These people sometimes perpetuate grief misconceptions, offer misguided advice and impose unrealistic and inappropriate expectations on the mourner. Though they do not do this knowingly, they in effect try to pull you off the path toward healing.

But there is a paradox in the concept of "understanding" grief. Yes, when the timing seems right and mourners are open to learning from those who have walked the path of loss before them, I try my best to provide information and education that helps them understand and affirms what they are experiencing. However, sometimes it is the very need to totally understand the experience of grief that can get you in trouble. For as someone once astutely observed, "Mystery is not something to be explained, it is something to be pondered."

1

Sometimes we simply cannot understand the death of someone we have loved so deeply. We cannot understand it now, and we will not understand it ever. I certainly couldn't understand why the doctors couldn't cure my dad's melanoma. I thought, "After all, it's only skin cancer." I didn't understand, I protested!

I have found that sometimes it is in staying open to the mystery and recognizing that we don't understand and can't control everything that surrounds us that understanding eventually comes. In fact, perhaps it is "standing under" the mysterious experience of death that provides us with a unique perspective: *We are not above or bigger than death.* Maybe only after exhausting the search for understanding why someone we love died can we discover a newly defined "why" for our own life.

In my experience, "understanding" comes when we *surrender*: surrender our need to compare our grief (it's not a competition); surrender our self-critical judgments (we need to be self-compassion-

"A life without surrender is a life without commitment."

Jerry Rubin

ate); and surrender our need to completely understand (we never will). The grief that touches our souls has its own voice and should not be compromised by our need for comparison, judgment, or even complete understanding. You see, surrender is not the same as resignation. Actually, surrendering to the unknowable mystery is a courageous choice, an act of faith, a trust in God and in ourselves! We can only hold this mystery in our hearts and surround ourselves with love.

The Ten Touchstones, The Role of Hope, and Remembering Your Heart

I have used the concept of touchstones in this book because it speaks to my heart. By definition, a touchstone is a standard or a norm against which to measure something. In this book I describe ten touchstones—or benchmarks—that are essential physical, emotional, cognitive, social, and spiritual actions for you to take if your goal is to heal in grief and to find continued meaning in life.

Think of your grief as a wilderness—a vast, mountainous, inhospitable forest. You are in the wilderness now. You are in the midst of unfamiliar and often brutal surroundings. You are cold and tired. Yet you must journey through this wilderness. To find your way out, you must become acquainted with its terrain and learn to follow the sometimes hard-to-find trail that leads to healing.

In the wilderness of your grief, the touchstones are your trail markers. They are the signs that let you know you are on the right path. I also like to think of touchstones as "wisdom teachings" that the many people who have taught me about their grief journeys have conveyed to me. When you learn to identify and rely on the touchstones, you will not get lost in your journey, even though the trail will often be arduous and you may at times feel hopeless. (At the beginning of each touchstone you will find photos I took on a recent hiking weekend in Colorado. You might use these photos to help yourself visualize the path through the wilderness of your grief and the touchstones that will show you the way.)

And even when you've become a master journeyer, and you know well the terrain of your grief, you will at times feel like you are backtracking and being ravaged by the forces around you. This, too, is the nature of grief. Complete mastery of a wilderness is not possible. Just as we cannot control the winds and the storms and the beasts in nature, we can never have total dominion over our grief.

But, if you do your work of mourning, if you become an intrepid traveler on your journey, if you strive to achieve these ten touch-

"Hope sees the invisible, feels the intangible, and achieves the impossible."

Anonymous

stones, I promise you that you will find your way out of the wilderness of your grief and you will learn to make the most of the rest of your precious life.

3

Hope is an equally important foundation to this book. Hope is an expectation of a good that is yet to be. It is an expression of the present alive with a sense of the possible. It is a belief that healing can and will occur. In honoring the ten touchstones, you are making an effort to find hope for your continued life. Through intentional mourning, you yourself can be the purveyor of your hope. You create hope in yourself by actively mourning the death and setting your intention to heal.

When you feel hopeless (and you probably will at times), you can also reach out to others for hope. Spend time in the company of people who affirm

> *"Light is known to exist by virtue of darkness. One is the chair upon which the other sits."*
>
> Anonymous

your need to mourn yet at the same time give you hope for healing. People who are empathetic, nonjudgmental, good listeners and who model positive, optimistic ways of being in the world will be your best grief companions. They will help resupply you with hope when your stores are running low. They will help you build divine momentum toward your eventual exodus from the wilderness of your grief.

I also insisted that the word "heart" be contained in the title of this book. Why? Because my years of learning from my own losses, as well as the losses of those who have trusted me to walk with them, have taught me that an open heart that is grieving is a "well of reception;" it is moved entirely by what it has perceived. Authentic mourning is an opportunity to embrace that open heart in ways that allow for and encourage our healing.

> *"The centerpiece of the integration of grief is not the mind, but the heart."*
>
> A.W.

Perhaps the most important truth I have learned is that healing in grief is heart-based, not head-based. Modern therapies sometimes separate the head from the heart; it's as if we should somehow be able to rationally think through our grief. I *heartily* disagree! Carl Jung taught us years ago that every psychological struggle is ultimately a matter of spirituality. The contents of this book encourage you to think, yes, but more importantly, to feel with your heart and your soul.

Did you know that the word *courage* comes from the Old French word for heart (*coeur*)? Your courage grows for those things in life that impact you deeply. The death of someone you treasure opens, or engages, your heart. Now you must take your heart, which has been engaged, and muster the courage to encounter the ten essential touchstones. Courage can also be defined as the ability to do what one believes is right, despite the fact that others may strongly and persuasively disagree. If this book helps you authentically mourn, some may try to shame you. So, go forth with courage.

This book, directed from my heart to your heart, is an invitation to go to that spiritual place inside yourself and, transcending our mourning-avoidant society and even your own personal inhibitions about grief, enter deeply into the journey. In many ways the path of the heart is an individual exploration into the wilderness, along unmarked and unlit paths. In part, my hope in this book is to provide you some light along your path.

> *"There are pains that cannot be contained in the mind — only in the heart."*
>
> Stephen Levine

Honoring Your Journey

I have attempted to convey in the following pages an "active empathy," encouraging you to be the expert regarding your own experience. You see, I have discovered a touchstone in my own personal walks into grief and in my "companioning" of fellow human beings: I can only help people when I encourage them to teach me about their unique journeys into grief.

You may consider this helping attitude strange. After all, as a professional grief counselor, am I not supposed to "treat" the

5

Companioning vs. Treating

The word "treat" comes from the Latin root word "tractare," which means "to drag." If we combine that with the word "patient" we can really get in trouble. "Patient" means passive long-term sufferer." So if as a grief counselor I treat patients, I drag passive long-term sufferers.

On the other hand, the word "companion," when broken down into its original Latin roots, means "messmate": com for "with" and pan for "bread." Someone you would share a meal with, a friend, an equal. I have taken liberties with the noun "companion" and made it into the verb "companioning" because it so well captures the type of helping relationship I support and advocate.

More specifically, for me . . .

- Companioning is about honoring the spirit; it is not about focusing on the intellect.
- Companioning is about curiosity; it is not about expertise.
- Companioning is about learning from others; it is not about teaching them.
- Companioning is about walking alongside; it is not about leading.
- Companioning is about being still; it is not about frantic movement forward.
- Companioning is about discovering the gifts of sacred silence; it is not about filling every painful moment with words.
- Companioning is about listening with the heart; it is not about analyzing with the head.
- Companioning is about bearing witness to the struggles of others; it is not about directing those struggles.
- Companioning is about being present to another person's pain; it is not about taking away the pain.
- Companioning is about respecting disorder and confusion; it is not about imposing order and logic.
- Companioning is about going to the wilderness of the soul with another human being; it is not about thinking you are responsible for finding the way out.

In your journey through grief, seek out the support of those who naturally adopt a "companioning" attitude toward you and avoid those who don't.

person who has come to me for help? No, not really. My experience has made me aware that thinking a trained counselor like myself should have all the answers for grieving people only complicates their experience. Some traditional grief therapies tend to be controlling. The counselor is supposed to be "in charge" and to know what is best for the person in grief. This treatment-oriented, prescriptive model, however, simply does not work effectively!

I invite, sometimes even challenge, counselors who visit my Center for Loss in Fort Collins, Colorado, to adopt a "companioning" and a "teach me" attitude with people in grief. By adopting this companioning philosophy, we as counselors are less likely to make inappropriate interpretations or judgments of the mourner's experiences. This approach helps ensure that when a person in grief expresses thoughts, feelings, or attitudes, we consciously avoid making evaluative reactions like, "That's right or wrong," "That shouldn't be," or worse yet, "That's pathological."

> "Your vision will be clear only when you look into your heart. Who looks outside, dreams. Who looks inside, awakens."
> Carl Jung

In sum, I have discovered that if I allow you to be my teacher, I not only become more helpful to you, but I am enriched and changed in meaningful ways in my own life. Likewise, if you as mourner conceive of yourself as the teacher or expert of your own grief—as the master of the journey that is your grief, you will feel empowered to own what you are feeling and not feel shamed by the sometimes judgmental responses of others. You will also learn to seek out the support of those who naturally adopt a "companioning" attitude toward you and avoid those who don't.

How to Use This Book

My purpose in the pages that follow is to provide an opportunity for you to learn about your own unique journey into the wilderness that is grief. As you have without doubt already discovered, grief is an intensely personal experience. No two people will ever grieve and mourn in the same way, even when they are mourning the death of the same person. Your own grief is unlike anyone else's, even though you will find you share many commonalities with others in grief. I hope you discover this book to be a "safe place" to embrace what you uniquely think and feel without fear of being judged.

One of the concerns I have about many books written about grief is that they try to tell you, the reader, what to think and feel. This book, however, is different in one important way: It allows and encourages you to explore how you think and feel right now. While it does describe ten essential touch-stones, you will find that each of these touchstones will be "lived" and experienced in different ways by different people. The key is not to fit your experience to the touch-stones but to fit the touchstones to your experience. The companion journal to this book (*The Understanding Your Grief Journal: Exploring the Ten Essential Touchstones*) even gives you a special place to write out your thoughts and feelings. Neither this book nor the journal attempt to prescribe how you should feel, because to integrate a death into your life demands that you embrace your own unique responses, thoughts, and feelings.

So, I invite you to read this book with an eye to gleaning from it only what makes sense to you and your unique journey. I also invite and encourage you to complete the companion journal. Journaling in grief is a powerful method for helping yourself heal. It allows you to express your grief outside of yourself, yet keep your innermost thoughts and feelings private.

If you don't have the journal, you may simply want to buy an inexpensive spiral notebook and make notes to yourself as you are reading this text. After reading each page or two, ask yourself how what you've read applies to your own grief, then write your answers in your notebook.

If you're not a journaler, that's OK, too. Not everyone feels comfortable expressing themselves through the written word.

Talking about what you're reading in this book with someone who cares and understands is another effective way to integrate the touchstones and do your work of mourning.

In Gratitude

I thank you for taking the time to read and reflect on the words that make up this book. It is people just like you who have been my teachers. I am also grateful to the thousands of people who have participated in my retreat learning experiences about grief and who have embraced the "companioning" philosophy I hold so dear. Most important, I thank those who have gone before me for teaching me that grief is a birthright of life and that giving and receiving love is the essence of having meaning and purpose in our lives.

If you find this book helpful, write to me about your journey and allow me to learn from you as I have from countless others who have been touched by the death of someone loved.

Touchstone One

Open to the Presence of Your Loss

"In every heart there is an inner room, where we can hold our greatest treasures and our deepest pain."
Marianne Williamson

Someone you love has died. In your heart, you have come to know your deepest pain. From my own experiences with loss as well as those of thousands of grieving people I have companioned over the years, I have learned that we cannot go around the pain that is the wilderness of our grief. Instead, we must journey all through it, sometimes shuffling along the less strenuous side paths, sometimes plowing directly into the dark center.

In opening to the presence of the pain of your loss, in acknowledging the inevitability of the pain, in being willing to gently embrace the pain, you in effect honor the pain. "What?" you naturally protest, "honor the pain?" Crazy as it may sound, your pain is the key that opens your heart and ushers you on your way to healing.

In many ways, and as strange as it may seem, this book is intended to help you honor your pain. Honoring means recognizing the value of and respecting. It is not instinctive to see grief and the need to openly mourn as something to honor, yet the capacity to love requires the necessity to mourn. To honor your grief is not self-destructive or harmful, it is self-sustaining and life-giving!

What is Healing in Grief?

To heal in grief is to become whole again, to integrate your grief into your self and to learn to continue your changed life with fullness and meaning. Experiencing a new and changed "wholeness" requires that you engage in the work of mourning. It doesn't happen to you; you must stay open to that which has broken you.

Healing is a holistic concept that embraces the physical, emotional, cognitive, social, and spiritual realms. Note that healing is not the same as *curing*, which is a medical term that means "remedying" or "correcting." You cannot remedy your grief, but you can reconcile it. You cannot correct your grief, but you can heal it.

You have probably been taught that pain is an indication that something is wrong and that you should find ways to alleviate the pain. In our culture, pain and feelings of loss are experiences most people try to avoid. Why? Because the role of pain and suffering is misunderstood. Normal thoughts and feelings after a loss are often seen as unnecessary and inappropriate.

You will learn over time that the pain of your grief will keep trying to get your attention until you have the courage to gently, and in small doses, open to its presence. The alternative—denying or suppressing your pain—is in fact more painful. I have learned that the pain that surrounds the *closed* heart of grief is the pain of living against yourself, the pain of denying how the loss changes you, the pain of feeling alone and isolated—unable to openly mourn, unable to love and be loved by those around you.

Instead of dying while you are alive, you can choose to allow yourself to remain open to the pain, which, in large part, honors the love you feel for the person who has died. As an ancient Hebrew sage observed, "If you want life, you must expect suffering." Paradoxically, it is gathering the courage to move toward the pain that ultimately leads to the healing of your wounded heart. Your integrity is engaged by your feelings and the commitment you make to honor the truth in them.

In part, this book will encourage you to be present to your multitude of thoughts and feelings, to "be with" them, for they contain the truth you are searching for, the energy you may be lacking, and the unfolding of your

Dosing Your Pain

While this touchstone seeks to help you understand the role of pain in your healing, I want to make sure you also understand that you cannot embrace the pain of your grief all at once. If you were to feel it all at once, you could not survive. Instead, you must allow yourself to "dose" the pain—feel it in small waves then allow it to retreat until you are ready for the next wave.

healing. Oh, and keep in mind, you will need *all* of your thoughts and feelings to lead you there, not just the feelings you judge acceptable. For it is in being honest with yourself that you find your way through the wilderness and identify the places that need to be healed.

EXPRESS YOURSELF: Go to *The Understanding Your Grief Journal* on p. 10.

Setting Your Intention to Heal

You are on a journey that is naturally frightening, painful, and often lonely. No words, written or spoken, can take away the pain you feel now. I hope, however, that this book will bring some comfort and encouragement as you make a commitment to embracing that very pain.

It takes a true commitment to heal in your grief. Yes, you are wounded, but with commitment and intention you can and will become whole again. Commitment goes hand in hand with the concept of 'setting your intention." Intention is defined as being conscious of what you want to experience. A close cousin to "affirmation," it is using the power of positive thought to produce a desired result.

Reconciling Your Grief

An important concept to keep in mind as you journey through grief is that of *reconciliation*. You cannot "get over" or "recover from" or "resolve" your grief, but you can reconcile yourself to it. That is, you can learn to incorporate it into your consciousness and proceed with meaning and purpose in your life. See Touchstone Nine for more on reconciliation.

We often use the power of intention in our everyday lives. If you have an important presentation at work, you might focus your thoughts in the days before the presentation on speaking clearly and confidently. You might envision yourself being well-received by your colleagues. You have set your intention to succeed in this presentation. By contrast, if you focus on the many ways your presentation could fail, and you succumb to your anxiety, you are much less likely to give a good presentation.

How can this concept of setting your intention influence your journey through grief?

When you set your intention to heal, you make a true commitment to positively influence the course of your journey. You choose between being what I call a "passive witness" or an "active participant" in your grief. I'm sure you have heard this tired cliché: Time heals all wounds. Yet, time alone has nothing to do with healing. To heal, you must be willing to learn about the mystery of the grief journey. It can't be fixed or "resolved," it can only be soothed and "reconciled" through actively experiencing the multitude of thoughts and feelings involved.

"Believe that life is worth living, and your belief will help you create the fact."

William James

The concept of intention-setting presupposes that your outer reality is a direct reflection of your inner thoughts and beliefs. If you can change or mold some of your thoughts and beliefs, then you can influence your reality. And in journaling and speaking (and praying!) your intentions, you help "set" them.

You might tell yourself, "I can and will reach out for support in my grief. I will become filled with hope that I can and will survive this loss." Together with these words, you might form mental pictures of hugging and talking to your friends and seeing your happier self in the future.

Setting your intention to heal is not only a way of surviving your loss (although it is indeed that!), it is a way of actively guiding your grief. Of course, you will still have to honor and embrace your pain during this time. By honoring the presence of your pain, by understanding the appropriateness of your pain, you are committing to facing the pain. You are committing yourself to paying attention to your anguish in ways that allow you to begin to breathe life into your soul again. That, my friend, is a very good reason to give attention to your intention. The alternative would be to shut down in an effort to avoid and deny your pain, which is to die while you are still alive.

Setting Your Intention: Spiritual Pessimism Versus Spiritual Optimism

In part, you can choose whether you intend to experience spiritual pessimism or spiritual optimism. For example, if you believe that God is vengeful and punishes us for our sins by causing the untimely death of someone we love, it will be next to impossible for you to make it through difficult times. Not only will you carry the pain of the loss, you will carry the guilt and blame about how sinful you are to deserve this in your life. By contrast, if you "set your intention" to be what I would call "spiritually optimistic," and believe that embracing the pain of your loss can lead to reconciliation, you can and will survive.

In this book I will attempt to teach you to gently and lovingly confront your grief. To not be so afraid to express your grief. To not be ashamed of your tears and profound feelings of sadness. To not pull down the blinds that shut out light and love. Slowly, and in "doses," you can and will return to life and begin to live again in ways that put the stars back into your sky.

EXPRESS YOURSELF: Go to *The Understanding Your Grief Journal* on p. 11.

Making Grief Your Friend

You cannot heal without mourning or expressing your grief outwardly. Denying your grief, running from it, or minimizing it only seems to make it more confusing and overwhelming. To lessen your hurt, you must embrace it. As strange as it may seem, you must make it your friend.

When I reflect on making grief my friend, I think about my father. Sometimes when I fully acknowledge that I'll never see my father physically on this earth again, I am engulfed by an overwhelming sadness. Then I, with intention, try to give attention to what comes next. Yes, I feel his absence, but I also feel his presence. I realize that while my father has been dead for almost four years, my love and admiration for him have continued to grow. With every day that passes, the love I have for my father grows larger, undeterred by the loss of his physical presence. My intention has been, and continues to be, to honor his presence, while acknowledging his absence. The beauty of this is that while I mourn, I can continue to love.

EXPRESS YOURSELF: Go to *The Understanding Your Grief Journal* on p. 13.

No Reward For Speed

Reconciling your grief does not happen quickly or efficiently. "Grief work" may be some of the hardest work you ever do. Because grief is work, it calls on your physical, emotional, cognitive, social, and spiritual energy.

"It does not matter how slowly you go, so long as you do not stop."

Confucious

Consequently, you must be patient with yourself. When you come to trust that the pain will not last forever, it becomes tolerable. Deceiving yourself into thinking that the pain does not even exist makes it intolerable. Spiritual maturity in your grief work is attained when you embrace a paradox—to live at once in the state of both encounter and surrender, to both "work at" and "surrender" to your grief.

As you come to know this paradox, you will slowly discover the soothing of your soul. Resist the need to try to figure everything out with your head, and let the paradox embrace you. You will find yourself wrapped up in a gentle peace—the peace of living at once in both *encounter* (your "grief work") and *surrender* (embracing the mystery of not "understanding").

EXPRESS YOURSELF: Go to *The Understanding Your Grief Journal* on p. 13.

"Doing Well" With Your Grief

In the lovely book *A Grief Observed*, C.S. Lewis wrote about his experiences after the death of his wife. He said, "An odd by-product of my loss is that I'm aware of being an embarrassment to everyone I meet...perhaps the bereaved ought to be isolated in special settlements like lepers." As Lewis so eloquently teaches, society often tends to make those of us in grief feel shame and embarrassment about our feelings of grief.

Shame can be described as the feeling that something you are doing is bad. And you may feel that if you mourn, then you should be ashamed. If you are perceived as "doing well" with your grief, you are considered "strong" and "under control." The message is that the well-controlled person stays rational at all times.

Combined with this message is another one. Society erroneously implies that if you, as a grieving person, openly express your feelings of grief, you are immature. If your feelings are fairly intense, you may be labeled "overly-emotional" or "needy." If your feelings are extremely intense, you may even be referred to as "crazy" or a "pathological mourner."

As a professional grief counselor, I assure you that you are not immature, overly-emotional, or crazy. But the societal messages surrounding grief that you may receive are! I often say that society has it backwards in defining who is "doing well" in grief and who is "not doing well."

So, we often have these inappropriate expectations of how "well" we should be doing with our grief. These expectations result from common societal messages that tell us to be strong in the face of grief. We are told to "carry on," "keep your chin up," and to "keep busy."

Often combined with these messages is an unstated, but strong belief that "You have a right not to hurt. So do whatever is necessary to avoid it." Dismiss this trite suggestion also. The unfortunate result is you may be encouraged to pop pills, avoid having a funeral ceremony, or deny any and all feelings of loss.

> *"To suppress the grief, the pain, is to condemn oneself to a living death. Living fully means feeling fully; it means being completely one with what you are experiencing and not holding it at arm's length."*
>
> Philip Kapleau

Naturally, if you avoid your pain, the people around you will not have to "be with" you in your pain or experience their own pain. While this may be more comfortable for them, it would prove to be unhealthy for you. The reality is that many people will try to shield themselves from pain by trying to protect you from it. Do not let anyone do this to you!

When your personal feelings of grief are met with shame-based messages, discovering how to heal yourself becomes more difficult. If you internalize these messages encouraging repression of grief, you may even become tempted to act as if you feel better than you really do. Ultimately, however, if you deny the emotions of your heart, you deny the essence of your life.

EXPRESS YOURSELF: Go to *The Understanding Your Grief Journal* on p. 14.

Grief Is Not a Disease

You have probably already discovered that no "quick-fix" exists for the pain you are enduring. But I promise you that if you can think, feel, and see yourself as an active participant in your healing, you will experience a renewed sense of meaning and purpose in your life. Grief is not a disease. To be human means coming to know loss as part of your life. Many losses, or "little griefs," occur along life's path. And not all your losses are as painful as others; they do not always disconnect you from yourself. But the death of a person you have loved is likely to leave you feeling disconnected from both yourself and the outside world.

"We have to do the best we can. This is our sacred human responsibility."

Albert Einstein

Yet, while grief is a powerful experience, so, too, is your ability to help in your own healing. In your willingness to: 1) read and reflect on the pages in this book; 2) complete the companion journal, at your own pace; and 3) participate in a support group with fellow grief companions, you are demonstrating your commitment and setting your intention to re-invest in life while never forgetting the one you have loved.

I invite you to gently confront the pain of your grief. I will try with all my heart to show you how to look for the touchstones on your journey through the wilderness of grief so that your life can proceed with meaning and purpose.

EXPRESS YOURSELF: Go to *The Understanding Your Grief Journal* on p. 14.

Touchstone Two

Dispel the Misconceptions About Grief

"Two roads diverged in a wood, and I –
I took the one less traveled by,
And that has made all the difference."
Robert Frost

As you journey through the wilderness of your grief, if you
mourn openly and authentically, you will come to find a path
that feels right for you, that is your path to healing. But
beware—others will try to pull you off this path. They will try
to make you believe that the path you have chosen is wrong—
even "crazy," and that their way is better.

The reason that people try to pull you off the path to healing is
that they have internalized some common misconceptions about
grief and mourning. And the misconceptions, in essence, deny
you your right to hurt and authentically express your grief. They
often cause unrealistic expectations about the grief experience.

As you read about this important touchstone, you may discover
that you yourself have believed in some of the misconceptions
and that some may be embraced by people around you. Don't

condemn yourself or others for believing in these misconceptions. Simply make use of any new insights you might gain to help you open your heart to your work of mourning in ways that restore the soul.

Misconception

A misconception is a mistaken notion you might have about something—in other words, something you believe to be true but isn't. Misconceptions about grief are common in our society because we tend not to openly mourn or talk about grief and mourning. You can see how we'd have misconceptions about something as "in the closet" as grief.

Misconception 1: Grief and mourning are the same thing.

Perhaps you have noticed that people tend to use the words "grieving" and "mourning" interchangeably. There is an important distinction, however. We as humans move toward integrating loss into our lives not just by grieving, but by mourning. You will move toward "reconciliation" (see p. 145) not just by grieving, but through active and intentional mourning.

Grief is the constellation of internal thoughts and feelings we have when someone we love dies. Think of grief as the container. It holds all of your thoughts, feelings, and images of your experience when you are bereaved. In other words, grief is the internal meaning given to the experience of loss.

Bereavement: "to be torn apart," "to have special needs," "to be robbed."

Mourning is when you take the grief you have on the inside and express it outside of yourself. Another way of defining mourning is "grief gone public" or "the outward expression of grief." Talking about the person who died, crying, expressing your thoughts and feelings through art or music, and celebrating special anniversary dates that held meaning for the person who died are just a few examples of mourning.

A major theme of this book is rooted in the importance of openly and honestly mourning life losses, in expressing your grief outside of yourself. Over time and with the support of others, to mourn is to heal.

WARNING: After someone you love dies, your friends may encourage you to "keep your grief to yourself." If you were to take this message to heart, the disastrous result would be that all of your thoughts and feelings would stay neatly bottled up inside you. A catalyst for healing, however, can only be created when you develop the courage to mourn publicly, in the presence of understanding, compassionate people who will not judge you. At times, of course, you will grieve alone, but expressing your grief outside of yourself is necessary if you are to slowly and gently move forward in your grief journey.

I think it's so interesting that many native cultures actually created vessels—usually baskets, pots, or bowls—that symbolically contained their grief. They would put these vessels away for periods of time, only to bring them out on a regular basis to help themselves mourn.

Another way to think about what these cultures were instinctively doing was dosing themselves with their grief. As I've said, grief must be embraced little by little, in small bits with breaks in between. This dosing helps you survive what would, if absorbed in its totality all at once, probably kill you.

When you don't honor a death loss by acknowledging it, first to yourself and then to those around you, the grief will accumulate. Then, the denied losses come flowing out in all sorts of potential ways (e.g., deep depression, physical complaints, difficulty in relationships, addictive behaviors), compounding the pain of your loss.

EXPRESS YOURSELF: Go to *The Understanding Your Grief Journal* on p. 18.

23

Misconception 2:
Grief and mourning progress in predictable, orderly stages.

Probably you have already heard about the "stages of grief." This type of thinking about dying, grief, and mourning is appealing, but inaccurate. The notion of stages helps people make sense of death, an experience that is usually not orderly or predictable. If we believe that everyone grieves by going through the same stages, then death and grief become much less mysterious and fearsome. If only it were so simple!

The concept of "stages" was popularized in 1969 with the publication of Elisabeth Kübler-Ross's landmark text, *On Death and Dying*. In this important book, Dr. Kübler-Ross lists the five stages of grief that she saw terminally ill patients experience in the face of their own impending death: denial; anger; bargaining; depression; and acceptance. However, Kübler-Ross never intended for her stages to be interpreted as a rigid, linear sequence to be followed by all mourners. Readers, however, have done just that, and the consequences have often been disastrous.

"We have to find ways to unlearn those things that screen us from the perception of profound truth."

Thomas Moore

As a grieving person, you will probably encounter others who have adopted a rigid system of beliefs about what you should experience in your grief journey. And if you have internalized this myth, you may also find yourself trying to prescribe your grief experience as well. Instead of allowing yourself to be where you are, you may try to force yourself to be in another "stage."

For example, the responses of disorganization, fear, guilt and explosive emotions may or may not occur during your unique grief journey. Or relief may occur anywhere along the way and invariably overlap another part of your response. Sometimes your emotions may follow each other within a short period of time; or, at other times, two or more emotions may be present simultaneously. *Remember—do not try to determine where you "should" be. Just allow yourself to be naturally where you are in the process.*

Everyone mourns in different ways. Personal experience is your best teacher about where you are in your grief journey. Don't think your goal is to move through prescribed stages of grief. As you read further in this book, you will find that a major theme is understanding that your grief is unique. That word means "only one." No one ever existed exactly like you before, and no one will ever be exactly like you again. As part of the healing process, *the thoughts and feelings you will experience will be totally unique to you.*

EXPRESS YOURSELF: Go to *The Understanding Your Grief Journal* on p. 20.

Misconception 3:
You should move away from grief, not toward it.

Our society often encourages prematurely moving away from grief instead of toward it. The result is that too many mourners either grieve in isolation or attempt to run away from their grief through various means.

During ancient times, stoic philosophers encouraged their followers not to mourn, believing that self-control was the appropriate response to sorrow. Today, well-intentioned but uninformed relatives and friends still carry on this long-held tradition. While the outward expression of grief is a requirement for healing, overcoming society's powerful message (repress!) can be difficult.

"We are healed of a suffering only by experiencing it in the full."

Marcel Proust

As a counselor, I am often asked, "How long should grief last?" This question directly relates to our culture's impatience with grief and the desire to move people away from the experience of mourning. Shortly after the death, for example, mourners are expected to be "back to normal."

Mourners who continue to express grief outwardly are often viewed as "weak," "crazy," or "self-pitying." The subtle message is "Shape up and get on with your life." The reality is disturbing: Far too many people view grief as something to be *overcome* rather than *experienced.*

These messages, unfortunately, encourage you to repress your thoughts and feelings about the death. By doing so, you may refuse to cry. And refusing to allow tears, suffering in silence, and "being strong" are often considered admirable behaviors. Many people have internalized society's message that mourning should be done quietly, quickly, and efficiently. Don't let this happen to you.

After the death of someone loved, you also may respond to the question, "How are you?" with the benign response, "I'm fine." In essence, you are saying to the world, "I'm not mourning." Friends, family, and coworkers may encourage this stance. Why? Because they don't want to talk about death. So if you demonstrate an absence of mourning behavior, it tends to be more socially acceptable.

This collaborative pretense about mourning, however, does not meet your needs in grief. When your grief is ignored or minimized, you will feel further isolated in your journey. Ultimately, you will experience the onset of "going crazy" syndrome. (See Touchstone Five.) Masking or moving away from your grief creates anxiety, confusion and depression. If you receive little or no social recognition related to your pain, you will probably begin to fear that your thoughts and feelings are abnormal.

Remember—society will often encourage you to prematurely move away from your grief. You must continually remind yourself that leaning toward, not away from, the pain will facilitate the eventual healing.

EXPRESS YOURSELF: Go to *The Understanding Your Grief Journal* on p. 22.

Misconception 4:
Tears of grief are only a sign of weakness.

Just yesterday morning I read a lovely, personalized obituary in my local newspaper. The obituary described a man who had done many things in his life, had made many friends, and had touched the lives of countless people. He died in his 60s of cancer. At the end of the obituary, readers were invited to attend his funeral service and were instructed to bring memories and stories but NO TEARS. I nearly choked on my Cheerios.

Tears of grief are often associated with personal inadequacy and weakness. The worst thing you can do, however, is to allow this judgment to prevent you from crying. While your tears may result in a feeling of helplessness for your friends, family, and caregivers, you must not let others stifle your need to mourn openly.

"Let my hidden weeping arise and blossom."
Rainer Maria Rilke

Sometimes, as you can see from the obituary I describe, the people who care about you may, directly or indirectly, try to prevent your tears out of a desire to protect you (and them) from pain. You may hear comments like, "Tears won't bring him back," or "He wouldn't want you to cry." *Yet crying is nature's way of releasing internal tension in your body, and it allows you to communicate a need to be comforted.*

While data is still limited, researchers suggest that suppressing tears may actually increase your susceptibility to stress-related disorders. It makes sense. Crying is one of the excretory processes. Perhaps like sweating and exhaling, crying helps remove waste products from the body.

The capacity to express tears appears to allow for genuine healing. In my experience counseling mourners, I have even observed changes in physical expression after crying. Not only do people feel better after they cry, they also seem to look better. Tension and agitation seem to flow out of their bodies.

"Life is made up of sobs, sniffles, and smiles, with sniffles predominating."
O. Henry

27

You must be vigilant about guarding yourself against this misconception. Tears are not a sign of weakness or inadequacy. In fact, your capacity to share tears is an indication of your willingness to do the work of mourning.

EXPRESS YOURSELF: Go to *The Understanding Your Grief Journal* on p. 23.

Misconception 5:
Being upset and openly mourning means you are being "weak" in your faith.

Watch out for those people who think that having faith and openly mourning are mutually exclusive. Sometimes people fail to remember those important words of wisdom: "Blessed are those who mourn, for they shall be comforted."

Above all, mourning is a spiritual journey of the heart and soul. If faith or spirituality are a part of your life, express it in ways that seem appropriate to you. If you are mad at God, be mad at God. Actually, being angry at God speaks of having a relationship with God in the first place. I've always said to myself and others, "God has been doing very well for some time now—so I think God can handle my anger." Grief expressed is often grief diminished.

Similarly, if you need a time-out from regular worship, don't shame yourself. Going to "exile" for a period of time often assists in your healing. If people try to drag you to a place of worship, dig your heels in and tell them you may go, when and if you are ready.

When and if you are ready, attending a church, synagogue or other place of worship, reading scripture, and praying are only a few ways you might want to express your faith. Or, you may be open to less conventional ways, such as meditating or spending time alone in nature.

Don't let people take your grief away from you in the name of faith.

EXPRESS YOURSELF: Go to *The Understanding Your Grief Journal* on p. 25.

Misconception 6:
When someone you love dies, you only grieve and mourn for the physical loss of the person.

When someone you love dies, you don't just lose the presence of that person. As a result of the death, you may lose many other connections to yourself and the world around you. Sometimes I outline these potential losses, or what we call "secondary losses," as follows:

Loss of self

- self	("I feel like part of me died when he died.")
- identity	(You may have to rethink your role as husband or wife, mother or father, son or daughter, best friend, etc.)
-self-confidence	(Some grievers experience lowered self-esteem. Naturally, you may have lost one of the people in your life who gave you confidence.)
- health	(Physical symptoms of mourning.)
- personality	("I just don't feel like myself...")

Loss of security

- emotional security	(Emotional source of support is now gone, causing emotional upheaval.)
- physical security	(You may not feel as safe living in your home as you did before.)

29

| - fiscal security | (You may have financial concerns or have to learn to manage finances in ways you didn't before.) |
| - lifestyle | (Your lifestyle has changed and no longer feels as safe.) |

Loss of meaning

- goals and dreams	(Hopes and dreams for the future can be shattered.)
- faith	(You may question your faith.)
- will/desire to live	(You may have questions related to future meaning in your life. You may ask, "Why go on...?")
- joy	(Life's most precious emotion, happiness, is naturally compromised by the death of someone we love.)

Allowing yourself to acknowledge the many levels of loss the death has brought to your life will help you continue to "stay open" to your unique grief journey.

EXPRESS YOURSELF: Go to *The Understanding Your Grief Journal* on p. 27.

Misconception 7:
You should try not to think about the person who died on holidays, anniversaries, and birthdays.

As with all things in grief, trying not to think about something that your heart and soul are nudging you to think about is a bad idea. On special occasions such as holidays, anniversaries such as wedding dates and the day the person died, and your birthday or the birthday of the person who died, it's natural for your grief to well up inside you and spill over—even long after the death itself.

It may seem logical that if you can only avoid thinking about the person who died on these special days—maybe you can cram your day so tight that you don't have a second to spare, then you can avoid some heartache. What I would ask you is this: Where does that heartache go if you don't let it out when it naturally arises? It doesn't disappear. It simply bides its time, patiently at first, then urgently, like a caged animal pacing behind the bars.

No doubt you have some family and friends who may attempt to perpetuate this misconception. Actually, they are really trying to protect themselves in the name of protecting you.

While you may feel particularly sad and vulnerable during these times,

"Sometimes when one person is missing the whole world seems depopulated."
Lamartine

remember—these feelings are honest expressions of the real you. Whatever you do, don't overextend yourself during these times. Don't feel you have to shop, bake, entertain, send cards, etc. if you're not feeling up to it.

Instead of avoiding these days, you may want to commemorate the life of the person who died by doing something he or she would have appreciated. On his birthday, what could you do to honor his special passions? On the anniversary of her death, what could you do to remember her life? You might want to spend these times in the company of people who help you feel safe and cared for.

EXPRESS YOURSELF: Go to *The Understanding Your Grief Journal* on p. 28.

Misconception 8:
After someone you love dies, the goal should be to "get over" your grief as soon as possible.

You may already have heard the question, "Are you over it yet?" Or, even worse, be told, "Well, you should be over it by now!" To think that as a human being you "get over" your grief is ludicrous! You don't get over it, you learn to live with it. You learn to integrate it into your life and into the fabric of your being.

We will talk more about this important distinction in Touchstone Nine. For now, suffice it to say that you never "get over" your grief. As you become willing to do the work of your mourning, however, you can and will become reconciled to it. Unfortunately, when the people around you think you have to "get over" your grief, they set you up to fail.

EXPRESS YOURSELF: Go to *The Understanding Your Grief Journal* on p. 30.

Misconception 9:
Nobody can help you with your grief.

We have all heard people say, "Nobody can help you but yourself." Or you may have been told since childhood, "If you want something done right, do it yourself." Yet, in reality, perhaps the most compassionate thing you can do for yourself at this difficult time is to reach out for help from others.

Think of it this way: Grieving and mourning may be the hardest work you have ever done. And hard work is less burdensome when others lend a hand. Life's greatest challenges—getting through school, raising children, pursuing a career—are in many ways team efforts. So it should be with mourning.

"There is no path so dark, nor road so steep, nor hill so slippery that other people have not been there before me and survived. May my dark times teach me to help the people I love on similar journeys."

Maggie Bedrosian

Sharing your pain with others won't make it disappear, but it will, over time, make it more bearable. By definition, mourning (i.e., the outward expression of grief) requires that you get support from sources outside of yourself. Reaching out for help also connects you to other people and strengthens the bonds of love that make life seem worth living again.

EXPRESS YOURSELF: Go to *The Understanding Your Grief Journal* on p. 32.

Misconception 10:
When grief and mourning are finally reconciled, they never come up again.

Oh, if only this were so. As your experience has probably already taught you, grief comes in and out like waves from the ocean. Sometimes when you least expect it, a huge wave comes along and pulls your feet right out from under you.

Sometimes heightened periods of sadness overwhelm us when we're in grief—even years after the death. These times can seem to come out of nowhere and can be frightening and painful. Something as simple as a sound, a smell or phrase can bring on what I call "griefbursts." My dad loved Frank Sinatra's music. I have griefbursts almost every time I hear Frank's voice.

Allow yourself to experience griefbursts without shame or self-judgment, no matter where or when they occur. Sooner or later, one will probably happen when you're surrounded by other people, maybe even strangers. If you would feel more comfortable, retreat to somewhere more private, or go see someone you know will understand, when these strong feelings surface. (For more on griefbursts, see p. 75.)

You will always, for the rest of your life, feel some grief over this death. It will no longer dominate your life, but it will always be there, in the background, reminding you of the love you had for the person who died.

EXPRESS YOURSELF: Go to *The Understanding Your Grief Journal* on p. 33.

Keep in mind that the misconceptions about grief and mourning explored in this chapter are certainly not all the misconceptions about grief and mourning. Use the space provided in *The Understanding Your Grief Journal* (p. 34) to note any other grief misconceptions you have encountered since the death of someone loved.

When surrounded by people who believe these misconceptions, you will probably feel a heightened sense of isolation. If the people who are closest to you are unable to emotionally and spiritually support you without judging you, seek out others who can. Usually, the ability to be supportive without judging is most developed in people who have been on a grief journey themselves and are willing to be with you during this difficult time. When you are surrounded by people who can distinguish the misconceptions of grief from the realities, you can and will experience the healing you deserve.

Now that we've reviewed the common misconceptions of grief, let's wrap up Touchstone Two by listing some of the "conceptions." These are some realities you can hold onto as you journey toward healing.

Realistic Expectations for Grief and Mourning

- You will naturally grieve, but you will probably have to make a conscious effort to mourn.
- Your grief and mourning will involve a wide variety of different thoughts and feelings.
- Your grief and mourning will impact you in all five realms of experience: physical; emotional; cognitive; social; and spiritual.
- You need to feel it to heal it.
- Your grief will probably hurt more before it hurts less.
- Your grief will be unpredictable and will not likely progress in an orderly fashion.
- You don't "get over" grief; you learn to live with it.
- You need other people to help you through your grief.
- You will not always feel this bad.

Touchstone Three

Embrace the Uniqueness of Your Grief

> *"At bottom every man knows well enough that he is a*
> *unique human being, only once on this earth; and by*
> *no extraordinary chance will such a marvelously*
> *picturesque piece of diversity in unity as he is ever be*
> *put together a second time."*
> Nietzche

The wilderness of your grief is *your* wilderness—it is a creation
of your unique self, the unique person who died, and the unique
circumstances of your life. Your wilderness may be rockier or
more level than others. Your path may be revealed in a straight
line, or, more likely, it may be full of twists and turns. In your
wilderness, you will encounter places that are meaningful only
to you and you will experience the topography in your own
way.

In life, everyone grieves. But their grief journeys are never
precisely the same. Despite what you may hear, you will do the
work of mourning in your own special way. Be careful about
comparing your experience with that of other people. Do not
adopt assumptions about how long your grief should last. Just

consider taking a "one-day-at-a-time" approach. Doing so allows you to mourn at your own pace.

This touchstone invites you to explore some of the unique reasons your grief is what it is—the "whys" of your journey through the wilderness. The whys that follow are not all the whys in the world, of course, just some of the most common. As you write out your responses in your companion journal, I believe you will discover an increased understanding of the uniqueness of your grief.

Why #1: Your relationship with the person who died

Your relationship with the person who died was different than that person's relationship with anyone else. For example, you may have been extremely close, or "best friends," as well as husband or wife. Or maybe your father was your "best bud" or your mother was your "cheerleader." Or if your child died, you are probably struggling with the loss of all the various aspects of the parent-child relationship. Perhaps you loved the person who died, but you had frequent disagreements or divisive conflicts. Or maybe you were separated by physical distance, so you weren't as close emotionally as you would have liked.

"God who loves rich variety...created not simply a single tree, but trees of all kinds, sizes, and shapes. Let me see the vast variety in ways of mourning."
Edward Hays

The stronger your attachment to the person who died, the more difficult your grief journey will be. It only makes sense that the closer you felt to the person who died, the more torn apart you will feel after the death. Ambivalent relationships can also be particularly hard to integrate after a death. You may feel a strong sense of "unfinished business"—things you wanted to say but never did, conflicts you wanted to resolve but couldn't or didn't.

Whatever the circumstances, you are the best person to describe and work toward understanding your relationship with the person who died.

EXPRESS YOURSELF: Go to *The Understanding Your Grief Journal* on p. 38.

Why #2: The circumstances of the death

How, why, and when the person died can have a definite impact on your journey into grief. For example, was the death sudden or anticipated? How old was the person who died? Do you feel you might have been able to prevent the death?

A sudden, unexpected death obviously does not allow you any opportunity to prepare yourself for what was about to happen. But are you ever "ready" for that moment at all? After a death due to terminal illness, friends and family members often tell me that they were still, in a sense, shocked by the death. I know this was my experience when my dad died. However, I did feel

> *"Even a happy life cannot be without a measure of darkness, and the word 'happy' would lose its meaning if it were not balanced by sadness."*
> Carl Jung

fortunate that I was able to share special time with him before he died and that we had ample opportunity to tell one another how we felt.

The age of the person who died also affects your acceptance of the death. Within the order of the world, we usually anticipate that parents will die before their children do. But when a child dies, this order of the world is turned upside-down. Or your grief might be heightened when a middle-aged person dies in what was thought to be the "prime of his life." Basically, we often find our grief easier when we feel that the person who died had a chance to live a full life. When we believe that the life was cut too short, our innate sense of injustice colors our grief.

You may also be asking yourself if you could have done anything to prevent the death. "If only I had gotten him to the doctor sooner," you may be thinking. Or, "If only I had driven instead of her." The "if-onlys" are natural for you to explore, even if there is no logical way in which you are responsible for the death. What you're really feeling, at bottom, is a lack of control over what happened. And accepting that we have little control over the lives of those we love is a difficult thing indeed.

EXPRESS YOURSELF: Go to *The Understanding Your Grief Journal* on p. 42.

Why #3: The ritual or funeral experience

Decisions you make relating to the funeral can either help or hinder your personal grief experience. There is no single, right way to have a funeral. We do know, however, that creating a meaningful ritual for survivors can aid in the social, emotional, and spiritual healing after a death.

The funeral is a time and a place to express your feelings about the death, thus legitimizing them. The funeral also can serve as a time to honor the person who has died, bring you closer to others who can give you needed support, affirm that life goes on even in the face of death, and give you a context of meaning that is in keeping with your own religious, spiritual, or philo-sophical background.

In many ways, the funeral is about creating divine momentum to help you convert your grief into mourning. A well-planned funeral also helps you "know what to do" when you do not know what to do.

If you were unable to attend the funeral of the person who died, or if the funeral was somehow minimized or distorted, you may find that this complicates your healing process. Be assured, however, that it is never too late after a death for you to plan and implement a ritual (even a second or third ceremony) that will help meet your needs. I call these "corrective emotional-spiritual experiences." You might choose to have a tree planting ceremony in the spring, for example, in honor of the person who died. Or you might elect to hold a memorial service on the anniversary of the death. The power of ceremony is that it helps people begin to heal. A meaningful funeral is really a good beginning, not, as you may have heard, "closure" or "the end." You deserve to have a meaningful ceremony, and so does the person who died.

EXPRESS YOURSELF: Go to *The Understanding Your Grief Journal* on p. 44.

Why #4: The people in your life

Mourning, as I have defined it in this book, requires the outside support of other human beings in order for you to heal. Without a stabilizing support system of at least one other person, the odds are that you will have difficulty in doing this work of mourning. Healing requires an environment of empathy, caring, and gentle encouragement.

"Walking with a friend in the dark is better than walking alone in the light."
Helen Keller

Sometimes other people may think that you have a support system when in fact you don't. For example, you may have family members or friends who live near you, but you discover that they have little compassion or patience for you and your grief. If so, a vital catalyst to healing is missing.

Or you also may have some friends and relatives who are supportive right after the death but who stop supporting you soon after. *Again, for healing to occur, social support must be ongoing.*

Even when you have a solid support system in place, do you find that you are willing and able to accept the support? If you are ashamed of your need to mourn, you may end up isolating yourself from the very people who would most like to walk with you in your journey through the wilderness of your grief.

EXPRESS YOURSELF: Go to *The Understanding Your Grief Journal* on p. 46.

Why #5: Your unique personality

What words would you use to describe yourself? What words would other people use to describe you? Are you serious? Silly? Friendly? Shy?

Whatever your unique personality, rest assured that it will be reflected in your grief. For example, if you are quiet by nature, you may express your grief quietly. If you are outgoing, you may be more expressive with your grief.

How you have responded to other losses or crises in your life may be consistent with how you respond to this death. If you tend to remain distant or run away from crises, you may do the same thing now. If, however, you have always confronted crises head-on and openly expressed your thoughts and feelings, you may now follow that pattern of behavior.

Other aspects of your personality, such as your self-esteem, values, and beliefs, also impact your response to the death. In addition, any long-term problems with depression or anxiety will probably influence your grief.

EXPRESS YOURSELF: Go to *The Understanding Your Grief Journal* on p. 49.

Why #6: The unique personality of the person who died

Just as your own personality is reflected in your grief journey, so, too, is the unique personality of the person who died. What was the person who died like? What role(s) did he or she play in your life? Was he the funny one? Or was she the responsible one?

Really, personality is the sum total of all the characteristics that made this person who he or she was. The way she talked, the way he smiled, the way she ate her food, the way he worked—all these and so many more little things go into creating personality. It's no wonder there's so much to miss and that grief is so complex when all these little things are gone all at once.

> *"After (her) death I began to see her as she had really been. It was less like losing someone than discovering someone."*
>
> Nancy Halle

Whatever you loved most about the person who died is what you will now likely miss the most. And paradoxically, whatever you liked least about the person who died is what may now trouble you the most. If, for example, your father was a cold, uncaring person, after his death you may find yourself struggling even more with his apparent lack of love. You may have always wished you could change this aspect of his personality, and now that he is gone, you know with finality that you can't.

Whatever your feelings are about the personality of the person who died, talk about them openly. *The key is finding someone you can trust who will listen to you without sitting in judgement of you.*

EXPRESS YOURSELF: Go to *The Understanding Your Grief Journal* on p. 51.

Why #7: Your gender

Your gender may not only influence your grief, but also the ways in which others relate to you at this time. While this is certainly not always true, men are often encouraged and expected to 'be strong" and restrained. Typically, men have more difficulty in allowing themselves to move toward painful feelings than women do.

Women sometimes have a hard time expressing feelings of anger. By contrast, men tend to be more quick to respond with explosive emotions. And because men are conditioned to be self-sufficient, they often resist accepting outside support.

We must be careful about generalizations, however. Sometimes too much is made of the differences between genders and not enough is made of the capacity to grieve and mourn. Willingness to mourn often transcends gender.

EXPRESS YOURSELF: Go to *The Understanding Your Grief Journal* on p. 56.

Why #8: Your cultural background

Your cultural background is an important part of how you experience and express your grief. Sometimes it's hard for modern-day North Americans to articulate what their cultural background is. "My mother is half Irish, a quarter Mexican and a quarter I don't know what," you might say. "And my father comes from a strong Italian family." So what does that make you? And how does this mixture influence your grief?

When I say culture, I mean the values, rules (spoken and unspoken), and traditions that guide you and your family. Often these values, rules, and traditions have been handed down generation after generation and are shaped by the countries or areas of the world your family originally came from. Education and political beliefs are also aspects of your cultural background (religion, too, but we'll get to that next).

Basically, your culture is your way of being in the world.

EXPRESS YOURSELF: Go to *The Understanding Your Grief Journal* on p. 57.

Why #9: Your religious or spiritual background

Your personal belief system can have a tremendous impact on your journey into grief. You may discover that your religious or spiritual life is deepened, renewed, or changed as a result of your loss. Or you may well find yourself questioning your beliefs as part of your work of mourning.

When someone loved dies, some people may feel very close to God or a Higher Power, while others may
"My religion is very simple. My religion is kindness."
Dalai Lama

feel more distant and hostile. You may find yourself asking questions such as, "Why has this happened to me?" or "What is the meaning of this?" You may not, however, find the answers to all of your questions about faith or spirituality.

The word "faith" means to believe in something for which there is no proof. For some people, faith means believing in and following a set of religious rules. For others, faith is a belief in God, a spiritual presence, or a force that is greater than we are.

Mistakenly, people may think that with faith, there is no need to mourn. If you buy into this misconception, you will set yourself up to grieve internally but not mourn externally. *Having faith does not mean you do not need to mourn. Having faith does mean having the courage to allow yourself to mourn.*

With the death of someone you love comes a "search for meaning" (we will explore more about this on p. 95). You will find yourself re-evaluating your life based on this loss. You will need someone who is willing to listen to you as you explore your religious or spiritual values, question your attitude toward life, and renew your resources for living. This process takes time, and it can lead to possible changes in your values, beliefs and lifestyle.

EXPRESS YOURSELF: Go to *The Understanding Your Grief Journal* on p. 58.

Why #10: Other crises or stresses in your life right now

What else is going on in your life right now? Although we often think it shouldn't, the world does keep turning after the death of someone loved. You may still have to work and manage finances. Other people in your life may be sick or in need of help of some kind. You may have children or elderly parents (or both!) to care for. You may have too many commitments and too little time and energy to complete them.

Whatever your specific situation, I'm sure that your grief is not the only stress in your life right now. And the more intense and numerous the stresses in your life, the more overwhelming your grief experience may be.

"Definition of courage: 'grace under pressure.'"
Ernest Hemingway

Take steps to de-stress your life for the time being, if at all possible. Now is the time to concentrate on mourning and healing in grief. Or, if you have extraordinarily difficult demands right now, such as the birth of a new baby or the start of a new job, you may need to slow down your grief and work on it in doses. This naturally delayed mourning is sometimes your only choice.

EXPRESS YOURSELF: Go to *The Understanding Your Grief Journal* on p. 60.

Why #11: Your experiences with loss and death in the past

One way to think about yourself is that you are the sum total of all that you have experienced in your life so far. Your consciousness is in large part a creation of what you do and what happens to you. Before this death, you may have experienced other significant losses in your life. Did anyone close to you die before? What was that death and subsequent grief journey like for you? How did it influence your expectations for future deaths in your life? Have you found those expectations to be true this time?

The more "experienced" you are with death, the less shocked you may feel this time around. Often people find that the more deaths they mourn, and the older they get, the more natural the cycle of life seems to them. This is not to say that they aren't sad and don't need to mourn. They are and they do. But it is to say that they begin to integrate death and loss more seamlessly into living.

Other non-death losses in your past may also influence your grief journey. Divorce, job loss, financial downturns, severed relationships—all these can affect your worldview as well as your capacity to mourn.

EXPRESS YOURSELF: Go to *The Understanding Your Grief Journal* on p. 62.

Why #12: Your physical health

How you feel physically has a significant effect on your grief. If you are tired and eating poorly, your coping skills will be diminished. If you are sick, your bodily symptoms may be as, if not more, pressing than your emotional and spiritual ones. We'll discuss this important issue further in the self-care chapter, p. 105. For now, bear in mind that taking care of yourself physically is one of the best things you can do to lay the foundation for healthy mourning.

EXPRESS YOURSELF: Go to *The Understanding Your Grief Journal* on p. 63.

Moving from Whys to Whats

What else has shaped your unique grief journey? There are probably other factors, large and small, that are influencing your grief right now. What are they? I invite you to think about them and to write about them in your companion journal.

EXPRESS YOURSELF: Go to *The Understanding Your Grief Journal* on p. 63.

The *"whys"* of your journey (the unique reasons your grief is what it is) may be helpful for you to consider, thus Touchstone Three. But what is even more fundamental for you to be attuned to is *what* your thoughts and feelings are. What are you feeling today? What have you been thinking about for the last day or two? A big part of healing in grief is learning to listen and attend to your inner voice and give expression to those thoughts and feelings as you experience them. In the next chapter we will discuss some of these common and varied feelings.

Touchstone Four

Explore Your Feelings of Loss

"Did you ever know, dear, how much you took away with you when you left? I was wrong to say the stump was recovering from the pain of the amputation. I was deceived because it has so many ways to hurt me that I discover them only one by one."

C.S. Lewis

On your journey through the wilderness of your grief, a critical trail marker to be on the watch for is Touchstone Four, which guides you in exploring your many and varied feelings of loss. Actually, this fourth touchstone colors all the others, because your emotions shape what each of the other touchstones *feels like* for you.

So far on the path to healing we've explored opening to the presence of your loss, dispelling the common misconceptions about grief, and embracing the uniqueness of your grief. The primary way in which you experience these touchstones is by how they feel for you. Opening to the presence of your loss creates pain and feels hurtful. It may also leave you feeling numb, angry, fatigued, as well as many other emotions.

Dispelling the common misconceptions about grief may cause you to feel relief and/or confusion. And embracing the uniqueness of your grief may ultimately give you a profound sense of peace.

As strange as your emotions may seem, they are a true expression of where you are right now. Rather than deny or feel victimized by your feelings, I want to help you learn to recognize and learn from them. Naming the feelings and acknowledging them are the first steps to dealing with them. It's actually this process of becoming friendly with your feelings that will help you heal.

This touchstone should help you see how normal your grief thoughts, feelings, and behaviors are. I have worked with thousands of grieving people and they have taught me about many, many different thoughts and feelings after a death. Rest assured that whatever your thoughts and feelings, while in one sense completely unique to you, they are also usually a common human response to loss. Questions throughout this section of your companion journal will encourage you to see if a particular feeling I am describing is, or has been, a part of your personal experience. Moreover, keep in mind that although you may not have experienced some of these thoughts and feelings so far, you may in the future.

Throughout this chapter you will also find a number of quotes by C.S. Lewis. They are all from his poignant and popular book *A Grief Observed*, which tells the story of his journey through grief after the death of his wife. If you haven't already, I urge you to read this book and think of C.S. Lewis as a companion in your journey.

Shock, Numbness, Denial, and Disbelief

"It feels like a dream," people in early grief often say. "I feel like I might wake up and none of this will have happened." They also say, "I was there, but yet I really wasn't. I managed to do what needed to be done but I didn't feel a part of it."

Thank goodness for shock, numbness, and disbelief! Other words that mourners use to describe their initial grief experience are *dazed* and *stunned*. These feelings are nature's way of temporarily protecting you from the full reality of the death. They help insulate you psychologically until you are more able to tolerate what you don't want to believe. In essence, these feelings serve as a "temporary time-out" or a "psychological shock absorber."

Especially in the beginning of your grief journey, your emotions need time to catch up with what your mind has been told. On one level, you know the person is dead. But on other, deeper levels, you are not yet able or willing to truly believe it. This mixture of shock, numbness, and disbelief acts as an anesthetic. The pain exists, but you may not experience it fully. Typically, a physiological component also accompanies feelings of shock. Your autonomic nervous system is affected and may cause heart palpitations, queasiness, stomach pain, and dizziness.

You may find yourself hysterically crying, fainting, having angry outbursts, or even laughing. These are all normal and necessary responses that help you survive right now.

Unfortunately, some people may try to squelch these behaviors, believing them to be hysterical, out-of-control, or abnormal. They may try to "quiet you" in an effort to feel more comfortable themselves. But this is an out-of-control, uncomfortable time for you. Trying to "control" yourself would mean suppressing your intuitive response to the loss. Don't do it. Remember—your needs are the priority right now, not theirs. Do what you need to do to survive.

"At other times it feels like being mildly drunk, or concussed. There is a sort of invisible blanket between the world and me. I find it hard to take in what anyone says."
C.S. Lewis

During your time of shock, you may not remember specific words being spoken to you. Your mind is blocking; it hears but does not listen. Although you may not remember some, or any, of the words other people are telling you, you may well remember that you felt comforted. Their nonverbal presence is probably more important to you than any words they might say.

Even after you have moved beyond the shock, numbness, and disbelief, don't be surprised if these feelings resurface. Birthdays, anniversaries, and other special occasions that may only be known to you often trigger shock. You may suddenly realize that this person you loved so very much is no longer there to share these days with.

Denial is one of the most misunderstood aspects of the grief journey. Temporarily, denial, like shock and numbness, is a great gift. It helps you survive. However, your denial should soften over time as you mourn and as you acknowledge, slowly and in doses, that the person you loved is truly dead. While denial is helpful—even necessary—early in your grief, ongoing denial clearly blocks the path to healing. If you cannot accept the reality of the death, you can never mourn it.

Usually in grief, denial goes on at one level of awareness while acknowledgment of the reality of the death goes on at another level. Your mind may approach and retreat from the reality of the death over and over again as you try to embrace and integrate the meaning of the death into your life. This back-and-forth process is normal. I describe it as "Evade ◄►Encounter." The key is not to get stuck on evade.

Self-Care Guidelines

A critical point to realize is that shock, denial, numbness, and disbelief are not feelings you should try to prevent yourself from experiencing. Instead, be thankful that this "shock absorber" is available at a time when you need it most. Be compassionate with yourself. Allow for this instinctive form of self-protection. This dimension of grief provides a much-needed, yet temporary, means of survival.

A primary self-care principle during this time is to reach out for support from caring friends, family, and caregivers you trust.

When you are in shock, your instinctive response is to have other people care for you. Let them. Let yourself be nurtured.

Accepting support does not mean being totally passive and doing nothing for yourself, though. Actually, having someone take over completely is usually not helpful. Given appropriate support and understanding, you will find value in doing for yourself. In other words, don't allow anyone to do for you what you *want* to do for yourself.

A few misguided people may try to "talk you out of" your denial. They will make comments like, "You just have to admit what has happened." While your ultimate healing does require acknowledging the reality of the death, this period of shock and numbness is probably not the time to embrace the full depth of your loss. If others insist on taking away your early need to deny the death, ignore or avoid them.

EXPRESS YOURSELF: Go to *The Understanding Your Grief Journal*, p. 66.

Disorganization, Confusion, Searching, Yearning

Perhaps the most isolating and frightening part of your grief journey is the sense of disorganization, confusion, searching, and yearning that often comes with the loss. These feelings frequently arise when you begin to be confronted with the reality of the death. As one mourner told me, "I felt as if I were a lonely traveler with no companion and worse yet, no destination. I couldn't find myself or anybody else."

This dimension of grief may give rise to the "going crazy syndrome." Mourners often say, "I think I'm going crazy." That's because in grief, thoughts and behaviors are different from what you normally experience. If you feel disorganized and confused, know that you are not

"It doesn't seem worth starting anything. I can't settle down."
C.S. Lewis

51

going crazy, you are grieving. (The "going crazy syndrome" will be explained in more detail in Touchstone Five.)

After the death of someone loved, you may feel a sense of restlessness, agitation, impatience, and ongoing confusion. It's like being in the middle of a wild, rushing river where you can't get a grasp on anything. Disconnected thoughts race through your mind, and strong emotions may be overwhelming.

You may express disorganization and confusion in your inability to complete tasks. You may start to do something but never finish. You may feel forgetful and ineffective, especially early in the morning and late at night, when fatigue and lethargy are most prominent. Everyday pleasures may not seem to matter anymore.

You also may experience a restless searching for the person who has died. Yearning and preoccupation with memories can leave you feeling drained. You might even experience a shift in perception; other people may begin to look like the person in your life who died. You might be at a shopping mall, look down a hallway, and think you see the person you loved so much. Or you might see a familiar car whiz past and find yourself following the car in hopes that the person who died is inside. Sometimes you might think you hear the garage door open and the person entering the house as he or she had done so many times before. If these experiences are happening to you, remember—you're not crazy!

"I am thinking of her nearly always."

C.S. Lewis

Visual hallucinations occur so frequently that they can't be considered abnormal. I personally prefer the term "memory picture" to hallucination. As part of your searching and yearning when you're in grief, you may not only experience a sense of the dead person's presence, but you also may have fleeting glimpses of the person across the room.

You may also dream about the person who died. Dreams can be an unconscious means of searching for this person. Be careful

not to over-interpret your dreams. Simply remain open to
learning from them. If the dreams are pleasant, embrace them;
if they are disturbing, find someone who'll understand to talk to
about them.

*"My heart and body are crying
out, come back, come back."*
C.S. Lewis

Other common experi-
ences during this time
include difficulties
eating and sleeping. You may experience a loss of appetite, or
find yourself overeating. Even when you do eat, you may be
unable to taste the food. Having trouble falling asleep and early
morning awakening are also common experiences associated
with this dimension of grief.

And finally, keep in mind that disorganization following loss
always comes before any kind of re-organization. While they
may seem strange, feelings of disorganization, confusion,
searching, and yearning are actually steppingstones on your
path toward healing.

Self-Care Guidelines

If disorganization, confusion, searching, and yearning are, or
have been, a part of your grief journey, don't worry about the
normalcy of your experience. A critically important point is to
never forget these reassuring words—you are not crazy!

The thoughts, feelings, and behaviors of this dimension do not
come all at once. They are often experienced in a wave-like
fashion. You may need to talk and cry for long periods of time.
At other times, you may just need to be alone. Don't try to
interpret what you think and feel. Just think and feel it.
Sometimes when you talk you may not think you make much
sense. And you may not. But talking it out can still be self-clari-
fying, even if at an unconscious level.

When you feel disoriented, talk to someone who will understand. To heal, grief must be shared outside of yourself. I hope
you have at least one person whom you feel understands and
will not judge you. That person must be patient and attentive

because you may tell your story over and over again as you work to embrace your grief. He or she must be genuinely interested in understanding you. If you are trying to talk about your disorganization and confusion—and the person with whom you are speaking doesn't want to listen, find someone who will better meet your needs.

During this time, discourage yourself from making any critical decisions like selling your house and moving to another community. With the judgment-making difficulties that naturally come with this part of the grief journey, ill-timed decisions might result in more losses. Go slow and be patient with yourself.

EXPRESS YOURSELF: Go to *The Understanding Your Grief Journal*, p. 69.

Anxiety, Panic, Fear

Feelings of anxiety, panic, and fear also may be a part of your grief experience. You may ask yourself, "Am I going to be OK? Will I survive this? Will my life have any purpose without this person?" These questions are natural. Your sense of security has been threatened, so you are naturally anxious.

As your head and heart miss the person who was a part of your life, panic may set it. Feelings of anxiety and fear often elicit thoughts about "going crazy." If you begin to think you are "abnormal," your level of fear may also increase.

A variety of thoughts and situations can increase your anxiety, panic, and fear. For example, you may be afraid of what the future holds or that other people in your life will die soon. You may be more aware of your own mortality, which can be scary. You may feel vulnerable, even unable to survive, without the person who died. You

> *"No one ever told me that grief felt so much like fear."*
> C.S. Lewis

may feel panicky about your inability to concentrate. For some, financial problems can compound feelings of anxiety.

Your sleep might be affected by fear at this time. Fears of overwhelming, painful thoughts and feelings that can come up in dreams may cause you difficulty with sleeping. Or you may be afraid of being alone again in bed when you are not used to sleeping by yourself. Again, these are natural, but usually temporary, ways that fear can be part of your grief.

While unpleasant, anxiety, panic, and fear are often normal components of the grief experience. The good news is that expressing them can help make them feel more tolerable. And knowing that they are temporary may help you during this trying time.

Self-Care Guidelines

If anxiety, panic, and fear are a part of your grief journey, you will need to talk about them to someone who will be understanding and supportive. Not talking about these feelings makes them so much more powerful and destructive.

Under no circumstances are you to allow your fears and anxieties to go unexpressed. If you don't talk about them, you may find yourself retreating from other people and from the world in general. Many grieving people become prisoners in their own homes. They repress their anxiety, panic, and fear, only to discover that these feelings are now repressing them. Don't let this happen to you. And if you are having true panic attacks, please see your physician right away.

EXPRESS YOURSELF: Go to *The Understanding Your Grief Journal*, p. 71.

Explosive Emotions

Anger, hate, blame, terror, resentment, rage, and jealousy are explosive emotions that may be a volatile yet natural part of your grief journey. It helps to understand that all these feelings are, fundamentally, a form of protest. Think of the toddler whose favorite toy is yanked out of his hands. This toddler wants the toy; when it's taken, his instinctive reaction may be to scream or cry or hit. When someone loved is taken from you, your instinctive reaction may be much the same.

Explosive emotions may surface at any time when someone you have loved dies. You cry out in anguish, "How could this happen? This isn't fair! I hate this!" You may direct these emotions at the person who died, at friends and family

members, at doctors, at people who haven't experienced loss, at God.

> *"Why is He (God) so present a commander in our time of prosperity and so very absent a help in time of trouble?"*
> C.S. Lewis

Unfortunately, our society doesn't understand how normal and necessary these feelings can be. Demonstrating emotional hurts is judged as wrong. The implicit message is that you should try to "keep it together." When you're raging or terrified, others may get upset. The intensity of your own emotions may even upset you. Still, you must give yourself permission to feel whatever you feel and to express those feelings. If you collaborate with the well-intentioned but misinformed people around you, your body, mind, and spirit will probably be damaged in the process.

Some people may tell you that explosive emotions are not logical. "Anger won't bring him back," they might say. "He didn't mean to die, so don't be mad at him." Watch out. You might find yourself buying into this rational thinking. That's just the problem—thinking is logical; feeling is not.

Another problem is that people oversimplify explosive emotions by talking only about anger. Actually, you may experience a whole range of intense feelings such as those listed above. Underneath these emotions are usually feelings of pain, help-lessness, frustration, fear, and hurt.

If explosive emotions are part of your journey (and they aren't for everyone), be aware that you have two avenues for expression—outward or inward. The outward avenue leads to healing;

the inward avenue does not. Keeping your explosive emotions inside leads to low self-esteem, depression, guilt, physical complaints, and sometimes even persistent thoughts of suicide. (This critically important information on suicidal thoughts and feelings will be explored more on p. 80.)

Experiencing explosive emotions is normal. They should, however, lessen in intensity and duration as you do the work of mourning. Again, I want to emphasize that the key is finding someone who will help you understand what you are feeling and allow you to embrace your grief.

"Who still thinks there is some device (if only he could find it) which will make pain not be pain. It doesn't really matter whether you grip the arms of the dentist chair or you let your hands lie in your lap. The drill still drills on."

C.S. Lewis

Remember—you can't go around your grief, or over it, or under it—you must go through it. I hope that as you journey through grief you will be surrounded by people who understand, support, and love you and will help you explore your explosive emotions without trying to stifle you.

Self-Care Guidelines

Explosive emotions must be expressed, not repressed or worse yet, totally denied. Don't prescribe these feelings for yourself but do be alert for them. You will need a supportive listener who can tolerate, encourage, and validate your explosive emotions without judging, retaliating, or arguing with you. The comforting presence of someone who cares about you will help you seek continued self-understanding of your grief experience.

Be aware, though, of the difference between the right to feel explosive emotions and the right to act out these emotions in harmful ways. It's OK, sometimes even necessary, to feel angry. But if you hurt others or yourself or destroy property, the people who care about you will need to set limits on your behavior. Also, remind yourself that explosive emotions can often indicate underlying feelings of pain, helplessness, frustration, fear, and hurt. Listen to your explosive emotions and you may discover the need to embrace what's beneath.

Keep telling yourself that explosive emotions are not good or bad, right or wrong. They just are. They are your feelings and they are symptoms of an injury that needs nurturing, not judging. Paradoxically, the way to diminish explosive emotions is to experience them, even if they feel irrational to you.

EXPRESS YOURSELF: Go to *The Understanding Your Grief Journal*, p. 72.

Guilt and Regret

Guilt, regret, and self-blame are common and natural feelings after the death of someone loved. You may have a case of the "if-onlys": If only I had helped him find a different doctor... If only I had been with her that night... If only I hadn't said...

If you find yourself experiencing these if-onlys, be compassionate with yourself. When someone you care about dies, it's natural to think about actions you could or could not have taken to prevent the death. But of course, you are not to blame. It's simply impossible to go through life in close relationships with other people without saying or doing something you later wish you could change.

While these feelings of guilt and regret are natural, they are sometimes not logical to those around you. When you express your guilt and regret, some people may say, "Don't be silly. There was nothing you could have done." Whether you could have done something or not is beside the point. The point is that you are feeling like you could have or should have and you need to express those feelings, however illogical.

Other aspects of guilt and regret after a death include:

• *Survivor guilt*

Sometimes being alive when someone you love has died can cause what's termed survivor guilt. Have you found yourself thinking, "How come he or she died and I survived?" This is a natural question. It may be a part of your grief experience. If it is, find someone who will be understanding and allow you to talk it out.

• *Relief-guilt*

You may naturally feel relief if someone you love dies after a long period of illness and suffering. But your feelings of relief can also make you feel guilty. "I shouldn't be feeling relieved," you may think.

Relief-guilt also occurs when you recognize that you will not miss certain aspects of the relationship you had with the person who died. For example, you may not miss how the person made fun of you or never cleaned up after himself. Or you won't miss being slightly late for church because he was always running behind schedule.

To *not* miss some things about the person who died is fine. Realize that this doesn't mean you didn't love the person. An understanding listener can help you explore this as part of your work of mourning.

• *Joy-guilt*

Like relief-guilt, joy-guilt is about thinking that happy feelings are bad at a time of loss. Experiencing any kind of joy after the death can make you feel guilty. One day you might find yourself smiling or laughing at something, only to chastise yourself for having felt happy for a minute. It's as if your loyalty to the person who died demands that you be sad all the time now that he or she is gone. That's not true, of course. As you do the work of mourning, your natural healing journey will allow you to start experiencing more and more joy and less and less pain. If you're feeling guilty about the joy, find someone to talk to about it.

• *Magical thinking and guilt*

Consciously or unconsciously wishing for the death of someone loved—and then having that "wish" come true!—can make you feel guilty. We call this "magical thinking," because, of course, your thoughts didn't cause the death.

At some point in your relationship, you may have thought, "I wish you would go away and leave me alone." Or, if the relationship was very difficult, you may even have had more direct thoughts about death ending the relationship. If so, you may now feel somehow responsible for the death. Know that all relationships have periods in which negative thoughts prevail. But your mind doesn't have the power to inflict death. If you are struggling with any of these thoughts, find someone to talk with who will be understanding and non-judgmental.

> *"Still, there's no denying that in some sense I 'feel better,' and with that comes at once a sort of shame, and a feeling that one is under a sort of obligation to cherish and foment and prolong one's unhappiness."*
>
> C.S. Lewis

• *Longstanding personality factors*

Some people have felt guilty their entire lives. I hope you're not one of them, but you may be. Why? Because some people learn early in life, typically during childhood, that they are responsible when something bad happens. When someone dies, it is just one more thing to feel guilty about. If all-encompassing guilt is part of your experience, seek out a professional counselor who can help you work on understanding the nature and extent of your feelings.

Whatever your unique feelings of guilt and regret, don't let them go unexpressed. They are a natural part of your journey, and like all dimensions of grief, they need to be explored. So don't try to make this journey alone! Find a compassionate partner who will walk with you and listen to you without judgment.

And I would be remiss if I did not note that some mourners are in fact partly or wholly responsible for the death of someone loved. If your accidental or intentional actions resulted in the death, please, seek help from an experienced, well-trained grief counselor. Your feelings of guilt and remorse will certainly complicate your grief journey and you will need assistance coping with these sometimes intense feelings.

Self-Care Guidelines

If any aspect of guilt and regret is a part of your grief experience, look for a compassionate, patient, and non-judgmental listener. If you feel it, acknowledge it and express it openly.

Don't allow others to explain your feelings away. While they may be trying to help you, this attitude will not allow you to "talk out" what you think and feel on the inside. When you explore these feelings of guilt and regret, you will come to understand the limits of your own responsibility.

As you express yourself, remember—you aren't perfect. No one is. Something happened that you wish had not. Someone you care about has died. At times, you will naturally go back and review if you could have said or done anything to change this difficult reality. Allow yourself this review time, but as you do so, be compassionate with yourself. Continue to remind yourself that there are some things in life you cannot change.

One of the worst things you could do is to ignore or repress feelings of guilt. Many physical and emotional problems will result if you try to push these feelings away without talking them out. If feelings of guilt or regret are complicating your healing, don't be ashamed to find a trained grief counselor.

EXPRESS YOURSELF: Go to *The Understanding Your Grief Journal*, p. 74.

Sadness and Depression

Sadness can be the most hurtful feeling on your journey through grief. We don't want to be sad. Sadness saps pleasure from our lives. Sadness makes us feel crummy. As Americans, our Constitution even says we have a right to life, liberty and "the pursuit of happiness."

But sadness is a natural, authentic emotion after the death of someone loved. Something precious in your life is now gone. Of course you are sad. Of course you feel deep sorrow. Allowing yourself to feel your sadness is in large part what your journey toward healing is all about. I suggest you say out loud right now, "I have every right to feel sad!"

Weeks, or often months, will pass before you are fully confronted by the depth of your sorrow. The slow-growing nature of this awareness is good. You could not and should not try to tolerate all of your sadness at once. Your body, mind, and spirit need time to work together to embrace the depth of your loss. Be patient with yourself. Surround yourself with loving people who will understand, not judge you.

You may find that certain times and circumstances make you more sad than others. Grieving people often tell me that weekends, holidays, family meals, and any kind of anniversary occasion can be hard. So can bedtime, waking up in the morning, awakening in the middle of the night, and arriving home to an empty house. These difficult times usually have a special connection to the person who died.

"The act of living is different all through. Her absence is like the sky, spread all over everything."
C.S. Lewis

Unfortunately, our culture has an unwritten rule that says while physical illness is usually beyond your control, emotional distress is your fault. In other words, some people think you should be able to "control" or subdue your feelings of sadness. Nothing could be further from the truth. Your sadness is a symptom of your wound. Just as physical wounds require attention, so do emotional wounds.

Paradoxically, the only way to lessen your pain is to move toward it, not away from it. Moving toward your sadness is not easy to do. Every time you admit to feeling sad, people around you may say things like, "Oh, don't be sad" or "Get a hold of yourself" or "Just think about what you have to be thankful for." Comments like these hinder, not help, your healing. If your heart and soul are prevented from feeling the sadness, odds are your body may be harmed in the process. You have been emotionally, physically, and spiritually injured. Now you must attend to your injury.

Occasionally, your feelings of sorrow can be overwhelming enough to be classified as "clinical depression." After all, grief and mourning share many symptoms with depression, including sleep disturbances, appetite changes, decreased energy, with-drawal, guilt, dependency, lack of concentration, and a sense of loss of control. You may be having a hard time functioning at home and at work, which may compound your feelings of isolation and helplessness. If you feel totally immobilized, please get help from understanding friends or a professional counselor. If you're unsure if you're experiencing normal grief or clinical depression, seek out help.

Thoughts of suicide also may occur during your grief journey. Hundreds of grieving people have shared with me thoughts like, "I wouldn't mind if I didn't wake up tomorrow." Comments like this reflect a need to further explore the depth of your sadness. It's natural to experience these passive and passing suicidal thoughts; it is not natural to want to or make plans to take your own life when someone in your life dies.

If you have been thinking of taking your own life, talk to a professional helper. Suicidal thoughts are sometimes an expres-sion of wanting to find relief from the pain of your grief. Yes, you have been injured and you hurt. But to help your injury heal, you must openly talk about what this death has meant for you.

A Special Note About Clinical Depression and Getting Help

For hundreds of years, most people viewed depression as a sign of physical or mental weakness, not as a real health problem. Following years of research, "clinical depression" is now recognized as a true medical disorder exacerbated by psychological and social stress. In fact, at some point in their lives, close to one-fourth of all North Americans will experience at least one episode of clinical depression.

There are a number of influences that can play a role in the development of depression, including genetics, stress (such as the death of someone you love), and change in body and brain function. Many people with clinical depression have abnormally low levels of certain brain chemicals and slowed cellular activity in areas of the brain that control mood, appetite, sleep, and other functions.

In many ways, depression and grief are similar. Common shared symptoms are feelings of sadness, lack of interest in usually pleasurable activities, and problems with eating and sleeping. The central difference is that while grief is a normal, natural, and healthy process, clinical depression is not.

These differences between grief and depression can be measured by how long the feelings last and to what extent your daily activities are impaired. Grief softens over time; clinical depression does not. After the numbing and chaotic early days and weeks of grief, your daily schedule begins to proceed as usual. If you are clinically depressed, you may be unable to function day-to-day.

Depression can complicate grief in two ways. It can create short-term symptoms that are more severe and debilitating than those normally associated with grief. In addition, clinical depression can cause symptoms of grief to persist longer than normal and potentially worsen. If you have concerns about the difference between grief and depression, seek out a trained caregiver who specializes in this area of caregiving.

I have created the table below to help both caregivers and lay people distinguish between grief and clinical depression. I suggest you review this information (placing a checkmark beside those areas that you believe apply to you).

Normal Grief	Clinical Depression
You have normal grief if you...	You may be clinically depressed if you...
__ respond to comfort and support.	__ do not accept support.
__ are often openly angry.	__ are irritable and complain but do not directly express anger.
__ relate your depressed feelings to the loss experience.	__ do not relate your feelings of depression to a particular life event.
__ can still experience moments of enjoyment in life.	__ exhibit an all-pervading sense of doom.
__ exhibit feelings of sadness and emptiness.	__ project a sense of hopelessness and chronic emptiness.
__ may have transient physical complaints.	__ have chronic physical complaints.
__ express guilt over some specific aspect of the loss.	__ have generalized feelings of guilt.
__ feel a temporary loss of self-esteem.	__ feel a deep and ongoing loss of self-esteem.

Here is the great news! Depression is something that help is available for. With appropriate assessment and treatment, approximately eight out of ten people with depression will find relief from their depression. This could include you!

If you even suspect you are clinically depressed, it is critically important that you take steps to get help. Untreated depression can raise your risk for a number of additional health problems. It also may prevent you from moving forward in your journey through grief. You deserve to get help so you can continue to mourn in ways that help you heal. Choose life!

EXPRESS YOURSELF: Go to *The Understanding Your Grief Journal*, p. 77.

Self-Care Guidelines

As you embrace your feelings of sadness, you will need the comfort of trusted people—close friends, loving family members, and sometimes compassionate professional helpers. Your feelings of sadness can leave you feeling isolated and alone. Consequently, you will need to talk them out with accepting and understanding people. Talk to them about the death and its meaning to you. You need people to validate what you feel. You need people who will sometimes walk with you—not behind or in front of you but beside you—on your path through the wilderness.

Keep talking until you have exhausted your capacity to talk. Doing so will help reconnect you with the world outside of yourself. Or if you can't talk it out, write it out! Paint it out! Sing it out! But get the feelings outside of yourself. And give yourself permission to cry—as often and as much as you need to. Tears can help you cleanse your body, mind, and spirit.

Most important, remember that temporary feelings of sadness and depression have value in your grief journey. Actually, depression is nature's way of allowing for a time-out while you heal the wounds of your grief. Depression slows down your body and prevents major organ systems from being damaged. Depression allows you to turn inward and slow down your spirit, too. It aids in your healing and provides time to slowly begin re-ordering your life. These natural feelings can ultimately help you move ahead, to assess old ways of being, and to make plans for the future.

EXPRESS YOURSELF: Go to *The Understanding Your Grief Journal*, p. 76.

Relief and Release

Sometimes you may feel a sense of relief and release when someone you love dies. The death may have brought relief from suffering, particularly following an illness that was long and debilitating. Your relief, then, is normal and natural. Understand that your relief does not equate to a lack of love for the person who died.

When you anticipate the death of someone who is terminally ill, you begin grieving and, I hope, mourning, long before the death itself. Your grief journey actually begins when the person you love enters the transition from living to dying. When you watch someone you love endure physical pain and loss of quality of life, you begin to understand that death can bring relief. And so when the death occurs, your feelings of relief may supercede all others for a time.

When someone dies who in life abused you (physically, sexually, or emotionally), you may feel a sense of relief that equates with a feeling of being safe for the first time. This is normal and appropriate.

Another form of relief you may experience comes when you finally express your thoughts and feelings about the death. If you have repressed or denied these feelings before, when you do express them you may feel as if a great pressure has been lifted from your head, heart, and soul.

"Something quite unexpected has happened...my heart is lighter than it has been for weeks."
C.S. Lewis

Allowing yourself to acknowledge relief as a part of your grief experience can be a critical step in your journey through grief. Working to embrace these feelings creates the opportunity to find hope in your healing.

Self-Care Guidelines

If you feel a sense of relief or release, write about it, or better
yet, talk it out. Again, find someone you trust who will listen
and hear you. If you feel guilty about being relieved, talk about
it with someone who can help you feel understood. Whatever
you do, don't isolate yourself. Talk about your feelings!

EXPRESS YOURSELF: Go to *The Understanding Your Grief
Journal*, p. 78.

A Final Thought About The Feelings
You May Experience

As you journey through the wilderness of your grief, over time
and with the support of others you will come to experience
what I like to describe as "reconciliation." When you come out
on the other side of the wilderness and you are able to fully
enjoy life and living again, you have achieved reconciliation of
your grief. You will learn more about this important concept in
Touchstone Nine. But before we get there, let's explore some of
the other trail markers to watch for on your path to healing.

Touchstone Five

Recognize You Are Not Crazy

"If you are sure you understand everything that is going on, you are hopelessly confused."
Walter Mondale

In all my years as a grief counselor, the most common question mourners have asked me is, "Am I going crazy?" The second most common question is, "Am I normal?" The journey through grief can be so radically different from our everyday realities that sometimes it feels more like being picked up and dropped onto the surface of the moon than it does a trek through the wilderness. The terrain is so very foreign and disorienting, and our behaviors in that terrain seem so out of whack, that we feel like we're going crazy.

I once counseled an older man whose wife had died. Before his wife's death, they frequently ran errands and drove places together in their car, he at the wheel and she in the passenger seat. Each time they parked outside their destination, the man would turn to his wife and ask, "Do you think we should lock the car?" and his wife would answer, "What's the point? We don't have anything worth stealing." Then, without further ado, they would get out of the car, lock it, and go into wherever they were going. This ritual had started early in their 50-year marriage and had continued until she died.

After her death, the husband continued to drive and do his errands. When he stopped and parked, his body would instinctively pivot to the right and he would start to say aloud, "Do you think we should..." Then he would cry and feel the pain of his loss. He would also wonder if he was going crazy.

In keeping with the principles of this book, the widower told his friends about his ongoing compulsion to turn to his wife and ask her if he should lock the car. He was expressing a part of his grief outside of himself and he was reaching out for help. But as too often happens in our mourning-avoidant society, instead of affirming that his searching and yearning were normal and that they were helping him encounter his grief and acknowledge the reality of the death, his friends told him he *was* going crazy and that he should see a grief counselor.

And so it was that he came to me. Rest assured that I helped this confused widower talk out his grief. I also normalized his car-locking ritual by helping him understand that it was helping him integrate the death. He wasn't going crazy! His instinct to continue to turn to his wife was very normal, and in grief, learning to follow your instincts is more than half the battle.

This man wasn't crazy, and you're not either. You may be experiencing thoughts and feelings that seem crazy because they are so unusual to you, but what is unusual in life is often usual in grief.

This touchstone helps you be on the lookout for the trail marker that affirms your sanity: Recognize You Are Not Crazy. It's an important trail marker, because if you miss it, your entire journey through the wilderness of your grief may feel like Alice's surreal visit to Wonderland. Actually, your journey may still feel surreal even if you find this trail marker, but at least you'll know in your head that you're not going crazy.

Following are a number of common thoughts and feelings in grief that cause mourners to feel like they're going crazy. They may or may not be a part of your personal experience. As I've said, my intent is not to prescribe what should be happening to you. Instead, I encourage you to become familiar with what you *may* encounter while you grieve and do your work of mourning.

Time Distortion

"I don't know what day it is, let alone what time it is!" This kind of comment is not unusual when you are mourning. Sometimes, time moves so quickly; at other times, it crawls. Your sense of past and future also may seem to be frozen in place. You may lose track of what day or even what month it is. Your inability to keep time right now isn't crazy. It's common in grief, particularly in the early days and weeks after the death.

"Whole years of joy glide unperceived away, while sorrow counts the minutes as they pass."
William Havard

EXPRESS YOURSELF: Go to *The Understanding Your Grief Journal*, p. 82.

Self-Focus

Especially early in your grief, you may find yourself being less conscious of the needs of others. You may not want to listen to other people's problems. You may not have the energy to attend to all the needs of your children or other family members. You may feel flabbergasted that the world is still turning while your life is at a complete standstill.

The compulsion to focus only on your own thoughts and feelings doesn't mean you're going crazy. What it does mean is that you need to focus on your self right now. Your mind and spirit are directing your attention away from others and into your self because you need this self-focus to integrate your grief. Don't feel guilty or selfish about these feelings. They are necessary for your survival. Later on you'll be ready to reconnect with others and support them in their life trials. Some people may try to take your grief away from you by trying to keep you from any kind of self-focus. They may want you to quickly re-enter the "regular" world because they don't understand your need for a temporary retreat. If turning inward is part of your experience, be assured you are normal.

The word *temporary* is important here. You may move back and forth between needing time alone and needing time with other people. If you stay only in a self-focused, inward mode, you may risk developing a pattern of not sharing your grief. As you well know by now, not sharing your grief will stunt your healing process.

When you are in pain following the death of someone loved, the turning inward and the need for self-focus is analogous to what occurs when you have a physical wound. You cover a physical wound with a bandage for a period of time. Then you expose the wound to the open air, which helps with healing but also risks contamination. The emotional, physical, and spiritual pain of grief certainly demands the same kind of protection.

EXPRESS YOURSELF: Go to *The Understanding Your Grief Journal*, p. 82.

Re-thinking and Re-telling the Story

Often when someone loved dies, you find yourself thinking about the circumstances of the death and the time immediately surrounding the death over and over again. You may feel like you can't "shake" your memories of certain moments. You may replay them repeatedly in your mind.

"To fashion an inner story of our pain carries us into the heart of it, which is where rebirth inevitably occurs."

Sue Monk Kidd

You may also feel the need—almost a compulsion– to tell other people about these prominent memories over and over again. You may find yourself wanting to talk about them all the time.

I call this process "telling the story." Telling the story isn't a sign that you're going crazy; in fact, it's a sign that you're doing your work of mourning. Whether you're conscious of this fact or not, you tell yourself the story and you tell others the story in an effort to integrate it into your life. What has happened to you—the death of someone you love—is so hard to fathom that your mind compels you to revisit it again and again until you've truly acknowledged it and embraced its presence. Telling the story helps bring your head and your heart together.

Allow yourself this necessary rumination. Blocking it out won't help you heal. Don't be angry with yourself if you can't seem to stop wanting to repeat your story, whether in your own mind or aloud to others.

Yes, it hurts to constantly think and talk about the person you loved so much. But remember—usually grief wounds get worse before they get better. Be compassionate with yourself. Try to surround yourself with people who allow and encourage you to repeat whatever you need to repeat. Support groups are helpful to many people because there is a mutual understanding of the need to "tell the story." Grace happens!

EXPRESS YOURSELF: Go to *The Understanding Your Grief Journal*, p. 83.

Sudden Changes in Mood

When someone loved dies, you may feel like you are surviving fairly well one minute and in the depths of despair the next. Sudden changes in your mood are a difficult, yet natural, part of your grief journey. These mood changes can be small or very dramatic. They can be triggered by driving past a familiar place, a song, an insensitive comment, or even a change in the weather.

Mood changes can make you feel like you're going crazy because your inappropriate self-expectation may be that you should follow a pattern of continual motion forward. In other words, you may expect yourself to keep feeling better and better. In reality, grief twists and turns like a mountainous trail. One minute you might be feeling great and the next, lousy.

If you have these ups and down, don't be hard on yourself. Be patient with yourself. As you do the work of mourning and move toward healing, the periods of hopelessness will be replaced by periods of hopefulness.

EXPRESS YOURSELF: Go to *The Understanding Your Grief Journal*, p. 84.

Powerlessness and Helplessness

Your grief can at times leave you feeling powerless. You may think or say, "What am I going to do? I feel so completely helpless." While part of you realizes you had no control over what happened, another part feels a sense of powerlessness at not having been able to prevent it. You would like to have your life back the way it was, but you can't. You may think, hope, wish, and pray the death could be reversed, but feel powerless in the knowledge that it can't.

"Death puts Life into perspective."
Ralph Waldo Emerson

Also, you may wonder that if somehow you or someone else would have acted differently or been more assertive, you could have prevented the death. Your "if onlys" and "what ifs" are often expressions of wishing you could have been more powerful or in control of something you could not. Lack of control is a difficult reality to accept, yet it is one that over time and through the work of mourning you must encounter. These feelings of helplessness and powerlessness in the face of this painful reality are normal and natural.

Almost paradoxically, by acknowledging and allowing for temporary feelings of helplessness, you help yourself. When you try to "stay strong," you often get yourself into trouble. Share your feelings with caring people around you. Remember—shared grief is diminished grief; find someone to talk to who will listen without judging.

EXPRESS YOURSELF: Go to *The Understanding Your Grief Journal*, p. 84.

Grief Attacks or Griefbursts

As one grieving father said, "I was just sailing along feeling pretty good, when out of nowhere came this overwhelming feeling of grief!" I call this a "griefburst," which is a sudden, sharp feeling of grief that can cause anxiety and pain. Some people call them grief attacks, because they attack you without warning.

You may think that long periods of deep depression make up the bulk of a typical grief journey. Actually, you may more frequently encounter acute and episodic "pangs" or "spasms" of grief in between relatively pain-free blocks of time.

During a griefburst, you may feel an overwhelming sense of missing the person you loved and find yourself openly crying, or perhaps even sobbing. As one woman told me, "I'll be busy for awhile, and sometimes even forget he has died. Then I'll see his picture or smell his favorite food, and I'll just feel like I can't even move."

"Grief comes in unexpected surges...mysterious cues that set off a reminder of grief. It comes crashing like a wave, sweeping me in its crest, twisting me inside out...then recedes."

Tony Talbot

Griefbursts may feel like "crazybursts," but they are normal. When and if one strikes you, be compassionate with yourself. You have every right to miss the person who has died and to feel temporary paralysis or loss of control. Whatever you do, don't try to deny a griefburst when it comes on. It is probably more powerful than you are.

I like to think of griefbursts as evidence that those we love are determined not to be forgotten. Although the pain of a grief attack hurts so deeply, allow it to wash over you. If you'd feel more comfortable, retreat to a private place where you can wail or scream or do whatever you need to do by yourself. Afterward, talk about your griefburst with someone who cares about you.

EXPRESS YOURSELF: Go to *The Understanding Your Grief Journal*, p. 85.

Crying and Sobbing

We already discussed the importance of tears of grief in Touchstone Two (see p. 27). But here I'd like to briefly revisit this topic as it pertains to your feelings of going crazy.

If you're crying and sobbing a lot, you may feel like you're out of control, which can trigger your feelings of going crazy. Sobbing is like wailing, and it comes from the inner core of your being. Sobbing is an expression of the deep, strong emotions within you. These emotions need to get out, and sobbing allows for their release.

In many Eastern cultures, sobbing and wailing (sometimes called *keening*) are encouraged and understood as a normal part of grief and mourning. In our culture, however, sobbing is often considered frightening. It is perceived as being "out of control." (That's where your feelings of loss of control come from!) But it is this very loss of control that helps you express your strong feelings. Your feelings are too strong to be under "control" inside you—and their authentic expression can't be under control, either.

"Weeping is perhaps the most human and universal of relief measures."

Karl Menninger

If you're crying or sobbing a lot, you're not crazy. Cry, wail, and sob as long and as hard and as often as you need to. Don't try to be strong and brave for yourself or others. Tears have a voice of their own. You will be wise to allow yours to speak to you. Listen to your tears and heal.

EXPRESS YOURSELF: Go to *The Understanding Your Grief Journal*, p. 85.

Borrowed Tears

Here's another kind of crying that can make you feel like you're going crazy: borrowed tears. Borrowed tears are tears that spring up when you are touched by something you might see, hear or smell, and you react with strong emotion. During a griefburst (see p. 75), you might be brought to tears by a place or a smell that directly reminds you of the person who died. Borrowed tears, on the other hand, seem to come out of nowhere and are triggered by something you don't associate with the person who died and wouldn't normally have been upset by.

Borrowed tears are called what they are called because you seem to be "borrowing" them from someone else's store of pain and memory. They're not yours! You might find yourself crying at a sappy commercial on TV or seeing a little bird out your window. These things never made you sad before. Why are you crying now?

You're crying because your heart and soul are hurting and your emotions are tender. Think of it this way: If you press on your leg gently with your hand, it doesn't hurt. But if you break your leg and then press on it, even the slightest touch can hurt. Your heart is broken now, and anything that touches your heart even slightly may hurt. This is normal and will pass as your heart is healed.

Linking Objects

Linking objects are items that belonged to the person who died that you now like to have around you. Objects such as clothing, books, knick-knacks, furniture, artwork, and other prized possessions can help you feel physically close to the person you miss so much.

Once when I was counseling a widow, she shared with me that she found it comforting to take one of her husband's shirts to bed with her. She said that as she clutched his shirt close to her, she didn't feel so alone. But as she worked with her grief over time, her need for the shirt dwindled.

If you like to hold, be near, look at, sleep with, caress, or even smell a special belonging of the person who died, you're not crazy. You're simply trying to hold on to a tangible, physical connection to the person. The person's body is no longer physically here, but these special items are. Like the woman who slept with her husband's shirt, you'll probably need your linking objects less and less over time, as you integrate the loss into your life. But you may always find these items special and you may always want to keep them.

> *"Death ends a life,*
> *not a relationship."*
> Jack Lemmon

Don't rush into giving away the belongings of the person who died, either. Sometimes people hurry into clearing out all the "stuff" because they think it will help them heal. It doesn't. In fact, getting rid of the belongings because they're too painful to have around is antithetical to the touchstones described in this book. Opening to the presence of the loss may include embracing the feelings that are stirred up by the belongings of the person who died. If you get rid of the belongings prematurely, you in effect rid yourself of a natural and necessary medium of healing.

I'd also like to point out the difference between cherishing some belongings and creating a "shrine." Mourners create a shrine when for years (sometimes decades) after the death they keep everything just as it was when the person died. Unlike keeping linking objects, creating a shrine often prevents you from acknowledging the painful new reality that someone you love has died. It's as if you expect the person to return to you at any moment.

I do think it's OK for mourners to leave the belongings of the person who died just as they were for a short time after the death, perhaps up to a year or so. In the early weeks and months of grief you may simply lack the energy to contend with the person's belongings and your feelings of shock and denial may, in some circumstances, be so powerful that you simply can't bring yourself to confront the person's clothing, furniture, keepsakes, etc. Within reason, go at your own pace. I often say that there are no rewards for speed, and that once you've disposed of something, you can't get it back.

EXPRESS YOURSELF: Go to *The Understanding Your Grief Journal*, p. 86.

Identification Symptoms of Physical Illness

When you care deeply about someone and they die, you sometimes develop new ways to identify and feel close to that person. One way is by relating to the physical symptoms of the person who died. For example, if she died from a brain tumor, you may have more frequent headaches. If he died from a heart attack, you may have chest pains. Of course, checking for organic problems is important, but you also should be aware that you might be experiencing identification symptoms of physical illness.

Grieving people have shared with me these examples:

"She had awful pains in her stomach, and after she died I began to have them, too. It kind of made me feel close to her. After awhile the stomach pain went away and I felt some sense of loss. As I have healed, I've been able to let go of the stomach pain."

"After my brother's heart attack and death, I began to have chest pains. I was scared so I went to the doctor for a check-up. He told me my heart was fine. Eventually, as my grief subsided, the chest pains did, too."

Don't be shocked if you have a few physical symptoms that are similar to those experienced by the person who died. You're not crazy. Your body is simply responding to the loss. As you do the hard work of mourning, however, these symptoms should go away. If they don't, find someone who will listen to you and help you understand what is happening.

EXPRESS YOURSELF: Go to *The Understanding Your Grief Journal*, p. 86.

Suicidal Thoughts

We touched on suicidal thoughts in Touchstone Four, but this subject is important enough to reemphasize here. Thoughts that come and go about questioning if you want to go on living can be a normal part of your grief and mourning. You might say or think, "It'd be so much easier to not be here." Usually this thought is not so much an active wish to kill yourself as it is a wish to ease your pain.

To have these thoughts is normal and not crazy; however, to make plans and take action to end your life is abnormal.

"Out of the ashes of our hopelessness comes the fire of our hope."

Anne Wilson Schaef

Sometimes your body, mind, and spirit can hurt so much that you wonder if you will ever feel alive again. Just remember that in doing the hard work of mourning, you can and will find continued meaning in life. Let yourself be helped as you discover hope for your healing.

If thoughts of suicide take on planning and structure, make certain that you get help immediately. Sometimes tunnel vision can prevent you from seeing choices. Please choose to go on living as you honor the memory of the person who died.

EXPRESS YOURSELF: Go to *The Understanding Your Grief Journal*, p. 87.

Drugs, Alcohol, and Grief

Unfortunately, when someone loved dies, you may be tempted to quickly quell your feelings of grief. This desire to avoid and to mask the pain is understandable. But inappropriately or indiscriminately using drugs and alcohol to help you do so only brings temporary relief from a hurt that must ultimately be embraced.

A well-meaning friend hands you a bottle of sleeping pills and says, "Take one tonight. You need your sleep." Or you find yourself sipping on the whiskey bottle to get through the day. Should you take these drugs?

First, never take prescription drugs unless they were prescribed for you by a medical doctor. One major study found that many people get their first medication when they are in grief from well-meaning friends and family. Don't do it! You don't know how you might react to a certain medication.

Don't take a drug that your doctor has prescribed, either, unless you understand and agree with the reasons for taking it and the effects it will have on you. If you need more information about why you are being told to take any kind of medication, ASK! Drugs that make you feel numb or unnaturally peaceful will only complicate your grief experience. After all, they will eventually wear off and you will still have to struggle with the pain. If your doctor has prescribed a drug to help you cope with your grief, you may want to get a second opinion.

Alcohol is yet another danger for grieving people. When you drink, you may indeed feel better—temporarily. But alcohol taken to mask painful feelings is only a crutch and may in fact cause an entirely new set of problems. Psychological or physical dependence can also be a problem with alcohol. If you or anyone around you has concerns about your alcohol consumption, get help from a trained chemical dependency counselor immediately.

This is not to say that grieving people should never take medication. You may, for example, become so exhausted from lack of sleep that *temporary* use of a sedative is warranted. And in some situations, tranquilizers or antidepressants are appropriate therapies for severe emotional reactions to trauma. It is important to note that people who were taking antidepressants prior to the death of someone loved should continue taking them afterwards as ordered by a physician. Their grief will not be further complicated by the use of these medications.

EXPRESS YOURSELF: Go to *The Understanding Your Grief Journal*, p. 87.

Dreams

Sometimes dreaming a lot about the person who died may contribute to your feelings of "going crazy." Mourners sometimes tell me that they can't stop thinking about the death—even in their sleep!

> *"Dreams are the touchstones of our character."*
> Henry David Thoreau

Keep in mind that dreams are one of the ways the work of mourning takes place. A dream may reflect a searching for the person who has died, for example. You may dream that you are with the person in a crowded place and lose him and cannot find him. Dreams also provide opportunities—to feel close to the person who died, to embrace the reality of the death, to gently confront the depth of the loss, to renew memories, or to develop a new self-identity. Dreams also may help you search for meaning in life and death or explore unfinished business. Finally, dreams can show you hope for the future.

The content of your dreams often reflects changes in your grief journey. You may have one kind of dream early in your grief and another later on. So if dreams are part of your trek through the wilderness, make use of them to better understand where you have been, where you are, and where you are going. Also, find a skilled listener who won't interpret your dreams for you, but who will listen to you!

"The dream reveals itself in its own timetable, but it does reveal itself."

Thomas Moore

On the other hand, you may experience nightmares, particularly after a traumatic, violent death. These dreams can be very frightening. If your dreams are distressing, talk about them with someone who can support and understand you.

EXPRESS YOURSELF: Go to *The Understanding Your Grief Journal*, p. 88.

Mystical Experiences

When someone you love dies, you may have experiences that are not always rationally explainable. That doesn't mean you're crazy! If you share these experiences with others, they may question your mental fitness. But I like to say that if you have mystical experiences, you're simply mystically sensitive.

The primary form of mystical experience that grieving people have taught me about is communicating with the person who died. Some people find the experience hard to believe and they try to explain it away in a rational manner: "I must have been dreaming" or "I was probably half-asleep." Others try to distance themselves from the experience because they are taught that such things are impossible: "A rational mind just doesn't experience those kinds of things." So, if you want to be considered "rational" or "sane" (and who doesn't!), you would feel compelled to distance yourself from this kind of "irrational" experience.

Mystical experiences vary greatly. In Alabama, for example, a mother whose daughter had died woke up one summer morning only to find it snowing in her back yard (and her back yard only)! The snow lasted for 15 minutes and then stopped. The mother understood this as a communication telling her that her daughter was all right and that she shouldn't worry so much. In another instance, a man whose wife had died saw her lying on the couch in his living room. "It's like she came to me and wrapped me in her arms. I felt warm and happy . . . I experienced her presence."

> *"It is this belief in a power larger than myself and other than myself which allows me to venture into the unknown and even the unknowable."*
>
> Maya Angelou

I have listened to and learned from hundreds of people who have seen, heard, and felt the presence of someone who has died. If you count yourself among this number, you're not going crazy. You can still be very sane and exceedingly rational while at times experiencing and embracing mystical encounters. Who on this earth is to say what's real and what isn't? Certainly not I. Remain open to these experiences and be thankful for the comfort they provide.

EXPRESS YOURSELF: Go to *The Understanding Your Grief Journal*, p. 88.

Anniversary and Holiday Grief Occasions

Naturally, anniversary and holiday occasions can bring about pangs of grief. Birthdays, wedding dates, holidays such as Easter, Thanksgiving, Hanukkah, and Christmas, and other special occasions create a heightened sense of loss. At these times, you may likely experience griefbursts.

Your pangs of grief also may occur in circumstances that bring up reminders of the painful absence of someone in your life. For many families, certain days have special meaning (for example, the beginning of spring, the first snowfall, an annual

Fourth of July party, or any time when activities were shared as a couple or a family), and the person who died is more deeply missed at those times.

If you're having a really tough time on special days, you're not crazy. Perhaps the most important thing to remember is that your feelings are natural. And sometimes the anticipation of an anniversary or holiday turns out to be worse than the day itself.

Interestingly, sometimes your internal clock will alert you to an anniversary date you may not consciously be aware of. If you notice you are feeling down or experiencing pangs of grief, you may be having an anniversary response. Take a look at the calendar and think about if this particular day has meant anything to you in years past.

Plan ahead when you know some naturally painful times are coming. Unfortunately, some grieving people will not mention anniversaries, holidays, or special occasions to anyone. So they suffer in silence, and their feelings of isolation increase. Don't let this happen to you. Recognize you will need support and map out how to get it!

EXPRESS YOURSELF: Go to *The Understanding Your Grief Journal*, p. 89.

You're Not Crazy, You're Grieving

Never forget that your journey through the wilderness of your grief may bring you through all kinds of strange and unfamiliar terrain. As I said at the beginning of this chapter, your experiences may seem so alien that you feel more like you're on the moon! When it seems like you're going crazy, remind yourself to look for the trail marker that assures you you're *not* going crazy. You're grieving. The two can feel remarkably similar sometimes.

Touchstone Six

Understand the Six Needs of Mourning

"Going to the woods and the wild place has little to do with recreation, and much to do with creation."
Wendell Barry

If you are hoping for a map for your journey through grief, none exists. Your wilderness is an undiscovered wilderness and you its first explorer.

But virtually all mourners who have journeyed before you have found that their paths are similar. There are more commonalities than there are differences. In an effort to describe these similarities, a number of authors have touted models of grief that refer to "stages." As we agreed in Touchstone Two about grief misconceptions, we do not go through orderly and predictable stages of grief with clear-cut beginnings and endings.

But when we are in mourning, we do basically have the same needs. Instead of referring to stages of grief, I say that we as mourners have six central needs. Remember I said in the Introduction that as we journey through grief, we need to follow the trail markers, or the touchstones, if we are to find our way out of the wilderness. The trail marker we will discuss in this chapter explores the six central needs of mourning. You might think of Touchstone Six as its own little grouping of trail markers.

You will find that several of the six needs of mourning reiterate and reinforce concepts found in other chapters of this book. I hope this reinforcement helps you embrace how very important these fundamental concepts are.

Throughout this chapter, you will also find a number of grief meditation passages that, when read slowly and thoughtfully, help you work on the corresponding need. These "reflections" are from my book *The Journey Through Grief: Reflections on Healing*. Many mourners have found this to be a healing, meditative text to read at bed-time or early morning time. I hope these excerpts will help you embrace the six needs of mourning.

Unlike the stages of grief you might have heard about, *the six needs of mourning are not orderly or predictable.* You will probably jump around in random fashion while working on them. You will address each need when you are ready to do so. Sometimes you will be working on more than one need at a time. Your awareness of these needs, however, will give you a participative, action-oriented approach to healing in grief as opposed to a perception of grief as something you passively experience.

The Six Needs of Mourning

1. Accept the reality of the death.
2. Let yourself feel the pain of the loss.
3. Remember the person who died.
4. Develop a new self-identity.
5. Search for meaning.
6. Let others help you—now and always.

Mourning Need 1:
Accept the Reality of the Death.

You can know something in your head but not in your heart. This is what often happens when someone you love dies. This first need of mourning, a close cousin to Touchstone One (open to the presence of your loss), involves gently confronting the reality that someone you care about will never physically come back into your life again.

It's as if the realness of what has happened waits around a corner. I don't want to make the turn, yet I know I must. Slowly, I gather the courage to approach.

Whether the death was sudden or anticipated, acknowledging the full reality of the loss may occur over weeks and months. You may expect him or her to come through the door, to call on the telephone, or even to touch you. To survive, you may try to push away the reality of the death at times. But to acknowledge that someone you love has died is a process, not an event; embracing this painful reality is not quick, easy, or efficient.

You may move back and forth between protesting and encountering the reality of the death. You may discover yourself replaying events surrounding the death and confronting memories, both good and bad. This replay is a vital part of this need of mourning. It's as if each time you talk it out, the event is a little more real.

To live into the future depends on my response to the reality of what I am experiencing. Temporarily, I need to create insulation from the full force of what I am coming to know. If I felt it all at once I might die. But feel it I must.

One moment the reality of the loss may be tolerable; another moment it may be unbearable. Be patient with this need. At times, you may feel like running away and hiding. At other times, you may hope you will awaken from what seems like a bad dream. As you express what you think and feel outside of yourself, you will be working on this important need.

Remember—this first need of mourning, like the other five that follow, may intermittently require your attention for months. Be patient and compassionate with yourself as you work on each of them.

EXPRESS YOURSELF: Go to *The Understanding Your Grief Journal* on p. 92.

Mourning Need 2:
Let Yourself Feel the Pain of the Loss.

Like Touchstone One (open to the presence of your loss), this need of mourning requires us to embrace the pain of our loss—something we naturally don't want to do. It is easier to avoid, repress or deny the pain of grief than it is to confront it, yet it is in confronting our pain that we learn to reconcile ourselves to it.

I may try to protect myself from my sadness by not talking about my loss. I may even secretly hope that the person who died will come back if I don't talk about it. Yet, as difficult as it is, I must feel it to heal it.

You will probably discover that you need to dose yourself in embracing your pain. In other words, you cannot (nor should you try to) overload yourself with the hurt all at one time. Sometimes you may need to distract yourself from the pain of the death, while at other times you will need to create a safe place to move toward it.

Feeling your pain can sometimes zap you of your energy. When your energy is low, you may be tempted to suppress your grief or even run from it. If you start running and keep running, you may never heal. Dose your pain: yes! Deny your pain: no!

Unfortunately, as I have said, our culture tends to encourage the denial of pain. We misunderstand the role of suffering. If you openly express your feelings of grief, misinformed friends may advise you to "carry on" or "keep your chin up." If, on the other hand, you remain "strong" and "in control," you may be congratulated for "doing well" with your grief. Actually, doing well with your grief means becoming well acquainted with your pain. Don't let others deny you this critical mourning need.

If you are a man, be aware that this need may be particularly difficult to meet. You may be conditioned to deny pain and encouraged to keep your feelings inside. You may expect yourself to "be strong" and "in control." Yet, despite your efforts at self-control, you may now be experiencing a variety of feelings at an intensity level you never thought possible. To slow down, turn inward and embrace hurt may be foreign to you. I hope you have caring friends who will be understanding, patient, and tolerant with you.

The grief within me has its own heartbeat. It has its own life, its own song. Part of me wants to resist the rhythms of my grief. Yet, as I surrender to the song, I learn to listen deep within myself.

As you encounter your pain, you will also need to nurture yourself physically, emotionally, cognitively, socially, and spiritually. Eat well, rest often, and exercise regularly. Find others with whom you can share your painful thoughts and feelings; friends who listen without judging are your most important helpers as you work on this mourning need. Give yourself permission to question your faith. It's OK to be angry with your God and to struggle with "meaning of life" issues at this time.

Never forget that grief is a process, not an event. Your pain will probably ebb and flow for months, even years; embracing it when it washes over you will require patience, support, and strength.

EXPRESS YOURSELF: Go to *The Understanding Your Grief Journal* on p. 93.

Mourning Need 3:
Remember the Person Who Died.

Do you have any kind of relationship with people after they die? Of course. You have a relationship of memory. Precious memories, dreams reflecting the significance of the relationship and objects that link you to the person who died (such as photos, souvenirs, clothing, etc.) are examples of some of the things that give testimony to a different form of a continued relationship. This need of mourning involves allowing and encouraging yourself to pursue this relationship.

The essence of finding meaning in the future is not to forget my past, as I have been told, but instead to embrace my past. For it is in listening to the music of the past that I can sing in the present and dance into the future.

The process of beginning to embrace your memories often begins with the funeral. The ritual offers you an opportunity to remember the person who died and helps to affirm the value of the life that was lived. The memories you embrace during the time of the funeral set the tone for the changed nature of the relationship. Even later on, meaningful rituals encourage the expression of cherished memories and allow for both tears and laughter in the company of others who loved the person who died.

Embracing your memories can be a very slow and, at times, painful process that occurs in small steps. Remember—don't try to do all of your work of mourning at once. Go slowly and be patient with yourself.

Some people may try to take your memories away. Trying to be helpful, they encourage you to take down all photos of the person who died. They tell you to keep busy or even to move out of your house. You, too, may think avoiding memories would be better for you. And why not? You are living in a culture that teaches you that to move away from—instead of toward—your grief is best.

Following are a few example of things you can do to keep memories alive while embracing the reality that the person has died:

- Talking out or writing out favorite memories.
- Giving yourself permission to keep some special keepsakes or "linking objects" (see p. 78).
- Displaying photos of the person who died.
- Visiting places of special significance that stimulate memories of times shared together.
- Reviewing photo albums at special times such as holidays, birthdays, and anniversaries.

Perhaps one of the best ways to embrace memories is through creating a "Memory Book" that contains special photographs you have selected and perhaps other memorabilia such as ticket stubs, menus, etc. Organize these items, place them in an album and write out the memories reflected in the photos. This book can then become a valued collection of memories that you can review whenever you want.

I can release the pain that touches my memories, but only if I remember them. I can release my grief, but only if I express it. Memories and grief must have a heart to hold them.

I also need to mention here the reality that memories are not always pleasant. If this applies to you, addressing this need of mourning can be even more difficult. To ignore painful or ambivalent memories is to prevent yourself from healing. You will need someone who can nonjudgmentally explore any painful memories with you. If you repress or deny these memories, you risk carrying an underlying sadness or anger into your future.

In my experience, remembering the past makes hoping for the future possible. Your future will become open to new experiences only to the extent that you embrace the past.

EXPRESS YOURSELF: Go to *The Understanding Your Grief Journal* on p. 94.

Mourning Need 4:
Develop a New Self-Identity.

Your personal identity, or self-perception, is the result of the ongoing process of establishing a sense of who you are. Part of your self-identity comes from the relationships you have with other people. When someone with whom you have a relationship dies, your self-identity, or the way you see yourself, naturally changes.

You may have gone from being a "wife" or "husband" to a "widow" or "widower." You may have gone from being a "parent" to a "bereaved parent." The way you define yourself and the way society defines you is changed. As one woman said, "I used to have a husband and was part of a couple. Now I'm not only single, but a single parent and a widow. . . I hate that word. It makes me sound like a lonely spider."

Now I realize: I knew myself so little. This death has forced me to become reacquainted with myself. I must slow down and listen.

A death often requires you to take on new roles that had been filled by the person who died. After all, someone still has to take out the garbage, buy the groceries, and balance the checkbook. You confront your changed identity every time you do something that used to be done by the person who died. This can be very hard work and, at times, can leave you feeling very drained of emotional, physical, and spiritual energy.

You may occasionally feel child-like as you struggle with your changing identity. You may feel a temporarily heightened dependence on others as well as feelings of helplessness, frustration, inadequacy, and fear. These feelings can be overwhelming and scary, but they are actually a natural response to this important need of mourning.

As you address this need, be certain to keep other major changes to a minimum if at all possible. Now is not the time for a major move or addition to the house. Your energy is already depleted. Don't deplete it even more by making significant changes or taking on too many tasks.

Remember—do what you need to do in order to survive, at least for now, as you try to re-anchor yourself. To be dependent on others as you struggle with a changed identity does not make you weak, bad, or inferior. Your self-identity has been assaulted. Be compassionate with yourself. Accept the support of others.

Many people discover that as they work on this need, they ultimately discover some positive aspects of their changed self-identity. You may develop a renewed confidence in yourself, for example. You may develop a more caring, kind, and sensitive part of yourself. You may develop an assertive part of your identity that empowers you to go on living even though you continue to feel a sense of loss. (To learn more about the self-identity changes that come with grief, see Touchstone Ten.)

When I have a commitment and longing to find my changed self, I have an alternative to the constant, blinding pain of the loss. Discovering my changed me clears a space to discover new life. I have something to turn toward instead of away from. I have something to cry out for that releases my inner tension. I have something that is authentic, real: It is the life that breaks through my loneliness, with a direction and power of its own. Welcome home.

EXPRESS YOURSELF: Go to *The Understanding Your Grief Journal* on p.100.

Mourning Need 5:
Search for Meaning.

When someone you love dies, you naturally question the meaning and purpose of life. You probably will question your philosophy of life and explore religious and spiritual values as you work on this need. You may discover yourself searching for meaning in your continued living as you ask "How?" and

95

"Why?" questions. "How could God let this happen?" "Why did this happen now, in this way?" The death reminds you of your lack of control. It can leave you feeling powerless.

The person who died was a part of you. This death means you mourn a loss not only outside of yourself, but inside of yourself as well. At times, overwhelming sadness and loneliness may be your constant companions. You may feel that when this person died, part of you died with him or her. And now you are faced with finding some meaning in going on with your life even though you may often feel so empty.

I must encounter my questions, my doubts, my fears. There is richness in these domains. As I explore them I don't reinforce my tensions but instead release them. In this way I transcend my grief and discover new life beyond anything my heart could ever have comprehended. Oh, the gentleness of new life.

This death calls for you to confront your own spirituality. You may doubt your faith and have spiritual conflicts and questions racing through your head and heart. This is normal and part of your journey toward renewed living.

You might feel distant from your God or Higher Power, even questioning the very existence of God. You may rage at your God. Such feelings of doubt are normal. Remember—mourners often find themselves questioning their faith for months before they rediscover meaning in life. But be assured: It can be done, even when you don't have all the answers.

I deserve to be proud of my search for meaning in life after the death of someone I love. Grief confronts me with the reality that life is now. Today. I can demonstrate the value in my life and the lives of those who have died by living them fully.

Early in your grief, allow yourself to openly mourn without pressuring yourself to have answers to profound "meaning of life" questions. Move at your own pace as you recognize that allowing yourself to hurt and finding meaning are not mutually exclusive. More often, your need to mourn and find meaning in your continued living will blend into each other, with the former giving way to the latter as healing occurs.

EXPRESS YOURSELF: Go to *The Understanding Your Grief Journal* on p. 102.

Mourning Need 6:
Let Others Help You—Now and Always.

The quality and quantity of understanding support you get during your work of mourning will have a major influence on your capacity to heal. You cannot—nor should you try to—do this alone. Drawing on the experiences and encouragement of friends, fellow grievers, or professional counselors is not a weakness but a healthy human need. And because mourning is a process that takes place over time, this support must be available months and even years after the death of someone in your life.

I heal, in part, by allowing others to express their love for me. By choosing to invite others into my journey, I move toward health and healing. If I hide from others, I hide from healing.

Unfortunately, because our society places so much value on the ability to "carry on," "keep your chin up," and "keep busy," many bereaved people are abandoned shortly after the event of the death. "It's best not to talk about the death," "It's over and done with," and "It's time to get on with your life" are the types of messages directed at grieving people that still dominate. Obviously, these messages encourage you to deny or repress your grief rather than express it.

If you know people who consider themselves supportive yet offer you these kinds of mourning-avoiding messages, you'll need to look to others for truly helpful support. People who see your mourning as something that should be "overcome" instead of experienced will not help you heal.

To be truly helpful, the people in your support system must appreciate the impact this death has had on you. They must understand that in order to heal, you must be allowed—even encouraged—to mourn long after the death. And they must encourage you to see mourning not as an enemy to be vanquished but as a necessity to be experienced as a result of having loved.

I need not instinctively know what to do or how to be with my grief. I can reach out to others who have walked this path before. I learn that to ultimately heal, I must touch and be touched by the experiences of those who have gone before me. These people can offer me hope, inner strength, and the gift of love.

Healing in your grief journey will depend not only on your inner resources, but also on your surrounding support system. Your sense of who you are and where you are with your healing process comes, in part, from the care and responses of people close to you. One of the important sayings of The Compassionate Friends, an international organization of grieving parents, is "You need not walk alone." I might add, "You cannot walk alone." You will probably discover, if you haven't already, that you can benefit from a connectedness that comes from people who also have had a death in their lives. Support groups, where people come together and share the common bond of experience, can be invaluable in helping you and your grief and supporting your need to mourn long after the event of the death.

You will learn more about support groups and how to create support systems for yourself later in this book. Right now, remind yourself that you deserve and need to have understanding people around you who allow you to feel your grief long after society deems appropriate.

EXPRESS YOURSELF: Go to *The Understanding Your Grief Journal* on p. 104.

Journeying With The Six Needs

I have been a grief educator for three decades and I've found that mourners are often helped by the concept of the six central needs of mourning. There is a lot of information in this book, but if you were to commit to memory one small piece of information, I would recommend that it be the six needs of mourning. Simply, upholding and fulfilling these six needs will help you heal. I would also encourage you to revisit this chapter time and again in the future and review your progress in meeting these needs.

Touchstone Seven

Nurture Yourself

"There is nothing in nature that can't be taken as a sign of both mortality and invigoration."
Gretel Ehrlich

I remind you that the word "bereaved," which to our modern-day ears can sound like an old-fashioned term only a funeral director might use, means "to be torn apart" and "to have special needs." So despite its obsolescence, the word is still accurate and useful. Perhaps your most important "special need" right now is to be compassionate with yourself. In fact, the word "compassion" means "with passion." Caring for and about yourself with passion is self-compassion.

This touchstone is a gentle reminder to be kind to yourself as you journey through the wilderness of your grief. If you were embarking on a hike of many days through the rugged mountains of Colorado, would you dress scantily, carry little water, and push yourself until you dropped? Of course not. You would prepare carefully and proceed cautiously. You would take care of yourself because if you didn't, you could die. The consequences of not taking care of yourself in grief can be equally devastating.

Over many years of walking with people in grief, I have discovered that most of us are hard on ourselves when we are in mourning. We judge ourselves and we shame ourselves and we take care of ourselves last. But good self-care is essential to your survival. Practicing good self-care doesn't mean you are feeling sorry for yourself, being selfish, or being self-indulgent; rather, it means you are creating conditions that allow you to integrate the death of someone loved into your heart and soul.

> "Climb the mountains and get their good tidings. Nature's peace will flow into you as sunshine flows into trees. The winds will blow their freshness into you, and the storms their energy, while cares will drop off like falling leaves."
>
> John Muir

I believe that in nurturing ourselves, in allowing ourselves the time and loving attention we need to journey safely and deeply through grief, we find meaning in our continued living. We have all heard the words, "Blessed are those who mourn, for they shall be comforted." To this I might add, "Blessed are those who learn self-compassion during times of grief, for they shall go on to discover continued meaning in life."

Remember—self-care fortifies your long and challenging grief journey, a journey which leaves you profoundly affected and deeply changed. Above all, self-nurturing is about self-acceptance. When we recognize that self-care begins with ourselves, we no longer think of those around us as being totally responsible for our well-being.

I also believe that self-nurturing is about celebration, about taking time to enjoy the moment, to find hidden treasures everywhere—a child's smile, a beautiful sunrise, a flower in bloom, a friend's gentle touch. Grief teaches us the importance of living fully in the present, remembering our past, and embracing our future.

Walt Whitman wrote, "I celebrate myself." In caring for yourself with passion, you are celebrating life as a human being who has been touched by grief and has come to recognize that the preciousness of life is a superb opportunity for celebration.

The Mourner's Code
Ten Self-Compassionate Principles

Though you should reach out to others as you journey through grief, you should not feel obligated to accept the unhelpful responses you may receive from some people. You are the one who is grieving, and as such, you have certain "rights" no one should try to take away from you.

The following list is intended both to empower you to heal and to decide how others can and cannot help. This is not to discourage you from reaching out to others for help, but rather to assist you in distinguishing useful responses from hurtful ones.

1. *You have the right to experience your own unique grief.*
   No one else will grieve in exactly the same way you do. So, when you turn to others for help, don't allow them to tell you what you should or should not be feeling.

2. *You have the right to talk about your grief.*
   Talking about your grief will help you heal. Seek out others who will allow you to talk as much as you want, as often as you want, about your grief. If at times you don't feel like talking, you also have the right to be silent.

3. *You have the right to feel a multitude of emotions.*
   Confusion, disorientation, fear, guilt, and relief are just a few of the emotions you might feel as part of your grief journey. Others may try to tell you that feeling angry, for example, is wrong. Don't take these judgmental responses to heart. Instead, find listeners who will accept your feelings without condition.

4. *You have the right to be tolerant of your physical and emotional limits.*
   Your feelings of loss and sadness will probably leave you feeling fatigued. Respect what your body and mind are telling you. Get daily rest. Eat balanced meals. And don't allow others to push you into doing things you don't feel ready to do.

5. You have the right to experience "griefbursts."
Sometimes, out of nowhere, a powerful surge of grief may overcome you. This can be frightening, but it is normal and natural. Find someone who understands and will let you talk it out.

6. You have the right to make use of ritual.
The funeral ritual does more than acknowledge the death of someone loved. It helps provide you with the support of caring people. More important, the funeral is a way for you to mourn. If others tell you the funeral or other healing rituals such as these are silly or unnecessary, don't listen.

7. You have the right to embrace your spirituality.
If faith is a part of your life, express it in ways that seem appropriate to you. Allow yourself to be around people who understand and support your religious beliefs.

8. You have the right to search for meaning.
You may find yourself asking, "Why did he or she die? Why this way? Why now?" Some of your questions may have answers, but some may not. And watch out for the clichéd responses some people may give you. Comments like, "It was God's will" or "Think of what you still have to be thankful for" are not helpful and you do not have to accept them.

9. You have the right to treasure your memories.
Memories are one of the best legacies that exist after the death of someone loved. You will always remember. Instead of ignoring your memories, find others with whom you can share them.

10. You have the right to move toward your grief and heal.
Reconciling your grief will not happen quickly. Remember, grief is best experienced in "doses." Be patient and tolerant with yourself. Avoid people who are impatient and intolerant with you. Neither you nor those around you must forget that the death of someone loved changes your life forever.

EXPRESS YOURSELF. Go to *The Understanding Your Grief Journal* on p. 108.

Nurturing Yourself in Five Important Realms

When we are "torn apart," one of our most important special
needs is to nurture ourselves in five important areas: physically,
emotionally, cognitively, socially, and spiritually. What follows
is a brief introduction to each of these areas. You will then be
invited to go to your companion journal and express how you
see yourself doing in each of these areas.

The Physical Realm

Your body may be letting you know it feels distressed. Actually,
one literal definition of the word "grievous" is "causing
physical suffering." You may be shocked by how much your
body responds to the impact of your loss.

Among the most common physical responses to loss are
troubles with sleeping and low energy. You may have difficulty
getting to sleep. Perhaps even more commonly, you may wake
up early in the morning and have trouble getting back to sleep.
During your grief journey, your body needs more rest than
usual. You may also find yourself getting tired more quickly—
sometimes even at the start of the day.

Sleeping normally after a loss would be unusual. If you think
about it, sleeping is the primary way in which we release
control. When someone in your life dies, you feel a loss of
control. You don't want to lose any more control by sleeping.
The need to stay awake sometimes relates to the fear of additional losses; therefore, you may stay awake because you want
to prevent more loss. Some grieving people have even taught
me that they stay awake hoping to not miss the person who died
in case he or she returns. If you have this experience, be assured
you are not crazy. It is a normal part of searching and yearning
for the person who died.

Muscle aches and pains, shortness of breath, feelings of
emptiness in your stomach, tightness in your throat or chest,
digestive problems, sensitivity to noise, heart palpitations,

queasiness, nausea, headaches, increased allergic reactions, changes in appetite, weight loss or gain, agitation, and generalized tension—these are all ways your body may react to the loss of someone loved.

If you have a chronic existing health problem, it may become worse. The stress of grief can suppress your immune system and make you more susceptible to physical problems.

Right now you may not feel in control of how your body is responding. Your body is communicating with you about the stress you are experiencing! Keep in mind, however, that in the majority of instances, the physical symptoms described above are normal and temporary.

Good self-care is important at this time. Your body is the house you live in. Just as your house requires care and maintenance to protect you from the outside elements, your body requires that you honor it and treat it with respect. The quality of your life ahead depends on how you take care of your body today. The "lethargy of grief" you are probably experiencing is a natural mechanism intended to slow you down and encourage you to care for your body.

"And no one ever told me about the laziness of grief."
C.S. Lewis

And be certain to "talk out" your grief. Many grieving people have taught me that if they avoid or repress talking about the death, their bodies will begin to express their grief for them.

Caring for Your Physical Self

The following "Twelve Commandments of Good Health" are good advice for anyone, but especially for anyone in mourning. While this is by no means an all-inclusive list, it should get you off to a good start. If you are procrastinating, adopt that now-famous Nike mantra, "Just do it!"

1. Stop smoking right now.

Smoking can kill you. Stopping smoking can add years to
your life. The main ways smoking kills is by heart disease,
lung disease, or cancer. Again, if you smoke you are being
self-destructive. It's poison, pure and simple. Tobacco kills
more than 350,000 Americans every year, making it the
leading cause of premature death in the United States. If
you can't stop on your own, get help.

2. Eat less fat.

Perhaps you realize you should eat less fat, but you eat it
anyway. Why? Because it tastes good and it's a habit. In
rebuttal: There are a lot of other things that taste good and
you can change bad habits. Fat clogs your arteries and
causes heart attacks and strokes.

My family physician wife, Susan, tells me that foods high
in saturated fats are the worst offenders. These foods also
tend to be high in cholesterol and do some of their damage
by building up plaque on the walls of your arteries. These
buildups are what leads to heart disease.

The reality is that the more your blood vessels are narrowed
by fat and cholesterol, the less oxygen will be circulated in
your body and the more fatigued you will feel. The
American Heart Association recommends getting no more
than 30 percent of your daily calories from fat. The less the
better.

3. Exercise your heart.

Think of your heart as an engine in your car. Let's say you
abuse it by driving it thousands of miles and never perform-
ing maintenance on it. And then one day in the middle of a
drive it just stops. Don't abuse your heart. It is the engine
that keeps you alive. Each day it beats one hundred
thousand times and pumps sixteen hundred gallons of blood
over sixty thousand miles of vessels. Your heart is your best
friend. Support it every chance you have.

One way to support your heart is to condition it. Aerobic conditioning trains your heart and your lungs so they can deliver more oxygen faster and more efficiently to the body. Just 30 minutes of exercise at least three times a week can keep your heart and lungs healthy. Do what you most enjoy. Walking, jogging, swimming, and cycling are very good forms of aerobic exercise.

4. Exercise your muscles.

The American College of Sports Medicine now recommends weight training for every adult. The earlier you start weight training, the more muscle you will keep in older age. Muscle conditioning is vitally important, yet often neglected.

There are two aspects to muscle fitness: endurance and strength. In a weight-training program, lifting lighter weights with more repetitions increases endurance, while lifting heavier weights with fewer repetitions increases strength. As you age, muscle strength declines more quickly than endurance.

The reality is that if you don't use your muscles, you will lose your muscles. Get help from a professional trainer to assist you in creating the right weight training program for you.

5. Exercise your mind and spirit.

The demands of grief—on top of your everyday commitments—prime you for plenty of stress. Building in some regular physical exercise lets you "get away" from the demands of an all-too-often hectic life. Exercise will help you experience an enhanced sense of well-being.

Exercise has a calming effect on the body and the mind. We know that people who regularly exercise say they handle pressure better, feel more confident, and are happier and less depressed than those people who don't exercise. In other words, exercise not only benefits the body, it benefits the mind and the spirit. Even if you think you are in great physical shape, exercise anyway.

6. Get adequate sleep.

Sleep is restorative. It allows you to live. Sleep allows your mind and body a chance to perform day-to-day maintenance and repairs. Choose to get enough sleep. Determine how much you need to feel your best and then make every effort to get it.

When possible, do try to go to bed at a similar time each night, and get up at a similar time each morning. Begin to move to completely relax an hour or so before you go to bed. Limit caffeine and alcohol intake.

7. Establish a relationship with a physician.

Making our health a priority requires creating a relationship with a trusted physician. Do you know that some people spend more time selecting a veterinarian for their pets than they do selecting a doctor for their bodies? That's if they pick a doctor at all.

Simple as it may seem, finding and making use of a good doctor can be one of the most practical choices you can make to leading a healthier and longer life. Think of physicians as coaches—trained professionals—who know how to help keep you healthy. If you don't already have one, find one now and work to create a health-partnership.

8. Slow down.

Being too busy to see a doctor is only one symptom of a fast-paced, hurry-up lifestyle. For many people, the feeling of being rushed permeates their entire life. Are you living out the "squeeze it all in" mentality? Are you simply too busy? Do you have to leave one commitment early to go to another?

If you can allow yourself to slow down, your perception will change. Life will become easier and more enjoyable. You will work smarter. You will discover that your quality of life is generated from within instead of being imposed from the outside. As you slow down you may find that much of what you previously thought was essential can actually be postponed, delegated, or even ignored. Instead of waiting to enjoy your life when everything is done, allow yourself to enjoy the journey.

9. Rest and relax.

Set aside time every day for some rest and relaxation —a minimum of thirty minutes. (I can hear some of you readers right now: "I just don't have time!") Don't fall into the trap of thinking your day off or weekend off are your time for rest and relaxation. You may find yourself running around trying to pack everything you haven't had time to do into this short time.

Build in rest and relaxation—and when you do, don't feel guilty. Your times of rest are every bit as important as your times of productivity. Remember, rest restores!

10. Stay fluid.

Many people aren't aware that one of the easiest ways to stay healthy is to drink lots of water. Think of water as the oil that lubricates the mind and the body. The universal recommendation is six to eight glasses (10-12 ounces each) of water a day.

11. Laugh—a lot.

It turns out that humor is good medicine. Research demonstrates that laughter stimulates chemicals in the brain that actually suppress stress-related hormones. Also, respiration and circulation are both enhanced through laughter.

If you're in grief, you may not feel like laughing very much right now. But as your journey progresses, find ways to build laughter into your life.

12. Invest in major relationships.

When it comes to your physical, emotional, and spiritual well-being, don't underestimate the importance of your family and friends. Whether it's your spouse, significant other, children, or close friends, the people you turn to for support can play an important role in your well-being.

Connected relationships with your family and friends can motivate you to take care of yourself—to eat right, exercise and get regular medical care. Your family and friends can be an important buffer from the stresses of everyday life. Yet, like a garden, family and friend relationships must be tended. You can't expect to get much, if anything, out of these relationships if you are too busy.

"Surround yourself with people who respect and treat you well."
Claudia Black

Slowing down from your busy life and spending time with family and friends will invite you to experience intimacy, play, compassion, respect, kindness, joy, and gratitude. If you are able to be truly present to your family and friends—without agendas, expectations, and preoccupations—you will feel more connected to each other by love.

EXPRESS YOURSELF. Go to *The Understanding Your Grief Journal* on p. 110.

The Emotional Realm

We explored in Touchstone Four a multitude of emotions that are often part of grief and mourning. These emotions reflect that you have special needs that require support from both outside yourself and inside yourself. Becoming familiar with the terrain of these emotions and practicing the self-care guidelines noted can

"The emotions may be endless. The more we express them, the more we may have to express."
E.M. Forster

and will help you authentically mourn and heal in small doses over time. The important thing to remember is that we honor our emotions when we give attention to them.

Caring for Your Emotional Self

Following are just a few ideas to help you care for your emotional self during your journey through grief. What ideas can you think of?

• *Reach out and touch.*

For many people, physical contact with another human being is healing. It has been recognized since ancient times as having transformative, healing powers. Have you hugged anyone lately? Held someone's hand? Put your arm around another human being? Hug someone you feel safe with. Kiss your children or a friend's baby. Walk arm in arm with a neighbor. You might also appreciate massage therapy. Try a session and see how it feels for you.

• *Listen to the music.*

Music can be very healing to mourners because it helps us access our feelings, both happy and sad. Music can soothe the spirit and nurture the heart. All types of music can be healing—rock & roll, classical, blues, folk. Do you play an instrument or sing? Allow yourself the time to try these activities again soon.

What music reminds you of the person who died? At first, listening to this special music may be too painful. But later you may find that playing music that reminds you of the person who died helps you keep her memory alive in your heart.

• *Draw a "grief map."*

The death of someone you love may have stirred up all kinds of thoughts and feelings inside you. These emotions may seem overwhelming or even "crazy." Rest assured that you're not crazy, you're grieving. Your thoughts and feelings—no matter how scary or strange they seem to you—are normal and necessary.

Sometimes, corralling all your varied thoughts and feelings into one place can make them feel more manageable. You could write about them, but you can also draw them out in diagram form. Make a large circle at the center of your map and label it GRIEF. This circle represents your thoughts and feelings since the death. Now draw lines radiating out of this circle and label each line with a thought or feeling that has contributed to your grief. For example, you might write ANGER in a bubble at the end of one line. Next to the word anger, jot down notes about why you feel mad.

Your grief map needn't look pretty or follow any certain rules. The most important thing is the process of creating it. When you're finished, explain it to someone who cares about you.

• *Schedule something that gives you pleasure each and every day.*

Often mourners need something to look forward to, a reason to get out of bed each morning. It's hard to look forward to each day when you know you will be experiencing pain and sadness. To counterbalance your normal and necessary mourning, each and every day plan—in advance—something you enjoy. Reading, baking, going for a walk, having lunch with a friend, gardening, playing computer games—do whatever brings you enjoyment.

EXPRESS YOURSELF. Go to *The Understanding Your Grief Journal* on p. 111.

The Cognitive Realm

Your mind is the intellectual ability to think, absorb information, make decisions and reason logically. Without doubt, you have special needs in the cognitive realm of your grief experience. Just as your body and emotions let you know you have experienced being "torn apart," your mind has also, in effect, been torn apart.

Thinking normally after the death of someone precious to you would be very unlikely. Don't be surprised if you struggle with short-term memory problems, have trouble making even simple decisions, and think you may

"Thinking is the talking of the soul with itself."
Plato

be going crazy. Essentially, your mind is in a state of disorientation and confusion.

Early in your grief, you may find it helpful to allow yourself to "suspend" all thought and purposefulness for a time. Allow yourself just to be. Your mind needs time to catch up with and process your new reality. In the meantime, don't expect too much of your intellectual powers.

In the Introduction, I discussed the importance of "setting your intention" to journey boldly through grief and heal. Your cognitive powers are quite remarkable. Willing yourself to think something can in fact help make that something come to be. Think about your desired reality and make it happen.

Caring for Your Cognitive Self

Following are just a few ideas to help you care for your cognitive self during your journey through grief. What ideas can you think of?

• *Ask yourself two questions: What do I want? What is wanted of me?*

The answers to these two questions may help you not only survive the coming months and years, but learn to love life again.

First, now that the person you love is gone, what do you want? What do you want to do with your time? Where do you want to live? With whom do you want to socialize? Whom do you want to be near? These are big questions that may take some time for you to answer.

Second, what is wanted of you? Who needs you? Who depends upon you? What skills and experience can you bring to others? What are you good at? Why were you put here on this earth? While considering what you want is important, it alone does not a complete life make.

Asking yourself these questions on a daily basis may help you focus on the here-and-now. What do I want from my life today? What is wanted of me today? Living in the moment will help you better cope with your grief.

• *Make a list of goals.*

While you should not set a particular time and course for your healing, it may help you to make other life goals for the coming year. Make a list of short-term goals for the next three months. Perhaps some of the goals could have to do with mourning activities (e.g., making a memory book or writing thank-you notes to people who helped at the time of the death).

Also make a list of long-term goals for the next year. Be both realistic and compassionate with yourself as you consider what's feasible and feels good and what will only add too much stress to your life. Keep in mind that, because of your grief, you may feel more fatigued than usual. Don't overcommit, thereby setting yourself up for failure.

Try to include at least one or two "just for fun" goals in your list. For example, you might want to take a photography class or learn to tie flyfishing flies.

• *But avoid making any major changes in your life for at least two years.*

While it can be helpful to have goals to help you look to a brighter future, it's a mistake to march too boldly ahead. Sometimes, in an effort to obliterate the pain and "move forward," mourners make rash decisions shortly after the death. Some move to a new home or city. Some quit their jobs. Some break ties with people in their life or take on new relationships too quickly.

Typically these changes are soon regretted. They often end up compounding feelings of loss and complicating healing as well as creating staggering new headaches. (For example, more than half of all remarriages within the first two years of widowhood end in divorce.)

If at all possible, avoid making drastic changes for at least two years after the death. You cannot run away from the pain, so don't make things worse by trying to. Instead, give yourself at least a full 24 months to consider any other major changes in your life.

Of course, sometimes you may be forced to make a significant change in your life soon after the death. Financial realities may force you to sell your house, for example. In these cases, know that you are doing what you must and trust that everything will work out.

• *Count your blessings.*

You may not be feeling very good about your life right now. You may feel that you are unlucky. You may feel you are destined to be unhappy. You may feel that the universe is conspiring against you. That's OK. There is, indeed, a time for every purpose under heaven—including self-doubt. Indeed, self-doubt is as normal a part of grief as anger or sadness.

Still, you are blessed. Your life has purpose and meaning, even without the presence of the person who died. It will just take you some time to think and feel this through for yourself.

Think of all you have to be thankful for. This is not to deny the hurt, for the hurt needs to take precedence right now. But it may help to consider the things that make your life worth living, too.

EXPRESS YOURSELF. Go to *The Understanding Your Grief Journal* on p. 113.

The Social Realm

The death of someone you love has resulted in a very real disconnection from the world around you. When you reach out and connect with your family and friends, you are beginning to reconnect. By being aware of the larger picture, one that includes all the people in your life, you gain some perspective. You recognize you are part of a greater whole—and that recognition can empower you. You open up your heart to love again when you reach out to others. Your link to family, friends, and community is vital for your sense of well-being and belonging.

"Call it a clan, call it a tribe, call it a family. Whatever you call it, whoever you are, you need one."

Jane Howard

If you don't nurture the warm, loving relationships that still exist in your life, you will probably continue to feel disconnected and isolated. You may even withdraw into your own small world and grieve, but not mourn. Isolation can then become the barrier that keeps your grief from softening over time. You will begin to die while you are still alive. Allow your friends and family to nurture you. Let them in and rejoice in the connection.

Caring for Your Social Self

Following are just a few ideas to help you care for your social self during your journey through grief. What ideas can you think of?

• *Recognize that your friendships will probably change.*

Mourners often tell me how surprised and hurt they feel when friends fall away after a death. "I found out who my friends really are," they say. Know that just as you are, your friends are doing the best they can. They surely still care about you, but they may also be grieving the death. And more to the point, they don't know how to be present to you in your pain. Grief is awkward. They may not even be conscious of this reaction, but nonetheless, it affects their ability to support you.

117

The best way for you to respond in the face of faltering friendships is to be proactive and honest. Even though you're the one who's grieving, you may need to be the one to phone your friends and keep in touch. When you talk to them, be honest. Tell them how you're really and truly feeling and that you appreciate their support. If you find that certain friends can't handle your "grief talk," stick to lighter topics with them and lean more heavily on the friends who can.

Over time, you will probably notice a natural attrition among your friends. You will need to grieve these losses, though you will likely also find that other friendships deepen and new ones emerge.

By contrast, maybe you are one of the fortunate people who feel tremendous support and love from your friends after a death. If so, rejoice that you have such wise and wonderful friends.

• *Find a grief "buddy."*

Though no one else will grieve this death just like you, there are often many others who have had similar experiences. We are rarely totally alone on the path of mourning. Even when there is no guide, there are fellow travelers.

Find a grief "buddy"—someone who is also mourning a death, someone you can talk to, someone who also needs a companion in grief right now. Make a pact with your grief buddy to call each other whenever one of you needs to talk. Promise to listen without judgment. Commit to spending time together. You might arrange to meet once a week for breakfast or lunch with your grief buddy.

• *Remember others who had a special relationship with the person who died.*

At times your appropriate inward focus will make you feel alone in your grief. But you're not alone. There are probably many other people who loved and miss the person who died. Think about

"Two in distress makes sorrow less."

Proverb

118

others who were affected by the death: friends, neighbors, distant relatives, caregivers. Is there someone outside of the primary "circle of mourners" who may be struggling with this death? Perhaps you could call her and offer your condolences. Or write and mail a brief supportive note. If you aren't a writer, give her a call or stop in for a visit.

EXPRESS YOURSELF. Go to *The Understanding Your Grief Journal* on p. 115.

The Spiritual Realm

When you are "torn apart," you may have many spiritual questions for which there are no easy answers: Is there a God? Why me? Will life ever be worth living again? That is why, if I could, I would encourage all of us when we are in the midst of grief to put down "Nurture my spirit" first on our daily to-do lists.

My own personal source of spirituality anchors me, allowing me to put my life into perspective. For me, spirituality involves a sense of connection to all things in nature, God, and the world at large. I recognize that, for some, contemplating a spiritual life in the midst of the pain of grief can be difficult.

Yet, life is a miracle and we need to remind ourselves of that, during both happy times and sad times. When it comes to our spiritual lives, we have an abundance of choices, all of which can be doors leading to the soul. Spirituality can be found in simple things: a sunrise or sunset; the unexpected kindness of a stranger; the rustle of the wind in the trees.

"To understand the restoration of the soul means we have to make spirituality a more serious part of everyday life."
Thomas Moore

If you have doubt about your capacity to connect with God and the world around you, try to approach the world with the openness of a child. Embrace the pleasure that comes from the simple sights, smells, and sounds that greet your senses. You can and will find yourself rediscovering the essentials within your soul and the spirit of the world around you.

Nurturing a spiritual life invites you to connect with nature and the people around you. Your heart opens and your life takes on renewed meaning and purpose. You are filled with compassion for other people, particularly those who have come to know grief. You become kinder, more gentle, more forgiving of others as well as yourself.

Caring for Your Spiritual Self

Following are just a few ideas to help you care for your spiritual self during your journey through grief. What ideas can you think of?

• *Create a sacred mourning space.*

Creating a sacred mourning space just for you may be one of the most loving ways you can help yourself heal. Yes, you need the support of other people, but nurturing yourself during difficult times can also involve going to "exile."

Whether it is indoors or out, give yourself a place for spiritual contemplation. The word contemplate means "to create space for the divine to enter." Think of your space, if only a simple room, as a place dedicated exclusively to the needs of the soul. Retreat to your space several times a week and honor your journey through grief.

• *Start each new day with a meditation or prayer.*

For many mourners, waking up in the morning is the hardest part of their day. It's as if each time you awaken you must confront anew the realization that the person you love so much has died.

Starting the day off with tears and a heavy heart, day in and day out, is so draining. Yet it may be a necessary part of your grief journey, especially in the early weeks and months after the death.

Later, however, you may begin to have the power to set the tone for your day by praying or meditating. When you wake up, stretch before getting out of bed. Feel the blood coursing through your body. Listen to the hum of your consciousness.

Repeat a simple phrase or prayer to yourself, such as: "Today I will live and love fully. Today I will appreciate my life." You might also offer words of gratitude: "Thank you, God, for giving me this day. Help me to appreciate it and to make it count."

• *Organize a tree planting.*

Trees represent the beauty, vibrancy, and continuity of life. A specially planted and located tree can honor the person who died and serve as a perennial memorial. You might write a short ceremony for the tree planting. (Or ask another family member to write one.) Consider a personalized metal marker or sign, too.

For a more private option, plant a tree in your own yard. Consult your local nursery for an appropriate selection. Flowering trees are especially beautiful in the spring. You might also consider a variety of tree that the person who died loved or that reminds you of a place that was special to the person who died.

• *Visit the great outdoors.*

For many people it is restorative and energizing to spend time outside. Mourners often find nature's timeless beauty healing. The sound of a bird singing or the awesome presence of an old tree can help put things in perspective.

Go on a nature walk. Or camping. Or canoeing. The farther away from civilization the better. Mother Earth knows more about kicking back than all the stress management experts on the planet—and she charges far less.

What was the favorite outdoor getaway of the person who died? It may be as awesome as a mountain peak or as simple as your own backyard. Wherever it is, go there if you can. Sit in quiet contemplation of your relationship. Offer up your thanks for the love you shared. Close your eyes and feel the person's spirit surround you.

• *Imagine the person who died in heaven.*

Do you believe in an afterlife? Do you hope that the person who died still exists in some way? Most mourners I've talked to—and that number runs into the tens of thousands—are comforted by a belief or a hope that somehow, somewhere, their loved one lives on in health and happiness. For some, this belief is grounded in religious faith. For others it is simply a spiritual sense.

If you do believe in an afterlife, you may feel like you can still have a kind of spiritual relationship with the person who died. You may still talk to her in the hopes that she can somehow hear you. You may send him unspoken messages every night when you go to bed. There is nothing wrong with trying to communicate with this person now and always—as long as your focus on this continued relationship doesn't prevent you from interacting with and loving people who are still alive.

If you believe in heaven, close your eyes and imagine what it might be like. Imagine the person who died strong and smiling. Imagine her waving to you. And imagine your reunion with her when, one day, you come to join her.

EXPRESS YOURSELF. Go to *The Understanding Your Grief Journal* on p. 116.

Practicing Self-Compassion

We've discussed the five realms of self-care in grief: physical, emotional, cognitive, social, and spiritual. If you care for yourself "with passion" in all five realms, you will find your journey through the wilderness much more tolerable. So be good to yourself.

Finding others who will be good to you on your journey is also critically important. You can't walk this path alone. In the next chapter we will help you construct a plan to reach out to others for help.

Touchstone Eight
Reach Out for Help

"Action is the antidote to despair."
Joan Baez

When someone you love dies, you must mourn if you are to renew your capacity for love. In other words, mourning brings healing. But healing also requires the support and understanding of those around you as you embrace the pain of your loss.

I've said that the wilderness of your grief is your wilderness and that it's up to you to find your way through it. That's true. But paradoxically, you also need companionship from time to time as you journey. You need people who will walk beside you and provide you with "divine momentum"—affirmations that what you are doing is right and necessary for you and will lead to your eventual healing. You do not need people who want to walk in front of you and lead you down the path they think is right, nor do you need people who want to walk behind you and not be present to your pain.

You've heard me urge you over and over again in this book to seek out the support of the people in your life who are naturally good helpers. A few solid shoulders to cry on and a handful of pairs of listening ears can make all the difference in the world. For something so difficult, it's fundamentally simple, really, this journey to healing.

Sharing your pain with others won't make it disappear, but it will, over time, make it more bearable. Reaching out for help also connects you to other people and strengthens the bonds of love that make life seem worth living again.

Where to Turn for Help

"There is strength in numbers," one saying goes. Another echoes, "United we stand, divided we fall." If you are grieving, you may indeed find strength and a sense of stability if you draw on an entire support system for help.

"When we admit our vulnerability, we include others. If we deny it, we shut them out."

May Sarton

Friends and family members can often form the core of your support system. Seek out people who encourage you to be yourself and who acknowledge your many thoughts and feelings about the death. What you need most now are caring, non-judgmental listeners.

In an ideal world, this is your family and friends. If this is not true for you, I encourage you to seek out other sources of support; get help from somebody else. Don't play the role of victim if your family and existing friends are not good grief companions.

You may also find comfort in talking to a minister or other religious leader. When someone loved dies, it is natural for you to feel ambivalent about your faith and question the very meaning of life. A clergy member who responds not with criticism but with empathy to all your feelings can be a valuable resource.

A professional counselor may also be a very helpful addition to your support system. In fact, a good counselor can be something friends and family members can't: an objective listener. A counselor's office can be that safe haven where you can "give voice" to those feelings you're afraid to express elsewhere. What's more, a good counselor will then help you constructively channel those emotions.

For many grieving people, support groups are one of the best helping resources. In a group, you can connect with others who have experienced similar thoughts and feelings. You will be allowed and gently encouraged to talk about the person who died as much and as often as you like.

Remember, help comes in different forms for different people. The trick is to find the combination that works best for you and then make use of it.

EXPRESS YOURSELF. Go to *The Understanding Your Grief Journal* on p. 120.

The Rule of Thirds

In my own grief journeys and in the lives of the mourners I have been privileged to counsel, I have discovered that in general, you can take all the people in your life and divide them into thirds when it comes to grief support.

One third of the people in your life will turn out to be truly empathetic helpers. They will have a desire to understand you and your unique thoughts and feelings about the death. They will demonstrate a willingness to be taught by you and a recognition that you are the expert of your experience, not them. They will be willing to be involved in your pain and suffering without feeling the need to take it away from you. They will believe in your capacity to heal.

> *"A faithful friend is the medicine for life."*
> The Apocrypha

Another third of the people in your life will turn out to be neutral in response to your grief. They will neither help nor hinder you in your journey.

And the final third of people in your life will turn out to be harmful to you in your efforts to mourn and heal. While they are usually not setting out intentionally to harm you, they will judge you, they will try to take your grief away from you, and they will pull you off the path to healing.

> "Piglet sidled up to Pooh from behind. 'Pooh,' he whispered. 'Yes, Piglet?' 'Nothing,' said Piglet. 'I just wanted to be sure of you.'"
>
> A.A. Milne

Seek out your friends and family members who fall into the first group. They will be your confidants and momentum-givers on your journey. When you are actively mourning, try to avoid the last group, for they will trip you up and cause you to fall.

EXPRESS YOURSELF. Go to *The Understanding Your Grief Journal* on p. 122.

How Others Can Help You
Three Essentials

While there are a multitude of ways that people who care about you might reach out to help you, here are three important and fundamental helping roles. Effective helpers will help you:

1. Embrace hope.
   These are the people around you who help you sustain the presence of hope as you feel separated from those things that make life worth living. They can be present to you in your loss, yet bring you a sense of trust in yourself that you can and will heal.

2. Encounter the presence of your loss.
   These are the people who understand the need for you to revisit and recount the pain of your loss. They help you "tell your story" and provide a safe place for you to openly mourn. Essentially, they give you an invitation to take the grief that is inside you and share it outside yourself.

3. Feel "companioned" in your journey.
These people serve as companions through whom your
suffering can be affirmed. They are able to break through
their separation from you and truly companion you where
you are at this moment in time. They know that real
compassion comes out of "walking with" you, not ahead of
you or behind you. The word grieve means "to bear a heavy
burden." Those who companion you in your grief realize
that as they help bear your burden of sorrow, they give you
hope that something good will be borne of it.

EXPRESS YOURSELF. Go to *The Understanding Your Grief
Journal* on p. 122.

Finding Help in a Crisis

If your feelings of grief are so overwhelming that you're afraid
your life or the life of someone in your care is in danger, you
are in crisis and should seek help immediately.

Signs of a crisis include:

• Thinking about, planning or attempting suicide.
• Failing to care for yourself (eating, bathing, dressing).
• Abusing alcohol or drugs

If any of these warning signs apply to you, call one of the
helping resources listed below without delay.

• Your local Crisis Hotline. Call information or look in the
  Yellow Pages.
• Your family physician.
• Your local hospital.
• Your community mental health center. Check your phone
  book's county government listings.
• 911.

How to Know if You Need Professional Help

Mourning is the normal expression of thoughts and feelings you experience when someone you love dies. It is a necessary, although painful, part of your grief journey. By openly embracing your pain, you will heal from your emotional wounds and reconcile this significant loss in a positive way. Some counselors refer to this process as "good" grief.

Some people find that seeing a counselor to facilitate this good grief process is helpful. A skilled professional can sometimes ease your grief journey and affirm that you are doing the right things to help yourself heal.

Good grief, however, can turn bad. If normal grief strays off course, the work of mourning can go on and on without the grieving person ever reaching reconciliation. It is a very good idea to find a trained bereavement counselor to help you if you are experiencing this "complicated" grief.

How can you tell if your grief is complicated? Any one of these factors could complicate your grief experience:

An unnatural or untimely death. Your grief might become complicated if the person you loved died suddenly or unexpectedly, or if the death was a suicide or a homicide.

Your personality. If you have unreconciled feelings or conflicts relating to other losses in your life, or if you have a tendency toward depression, you may be more susceptible to a complicated grief experience. Difficulties in expressing and managing feelings of sadness and anger, extreme dependency on the approval of others, or a tendency to assume too much responsibility also may complicate your grief journey.

Your relationship with the person who died. An intensely close relationship to the person who died may trigger complicated grieving, as might unreconciled conflicts with that person.

130

An inability to express your grief. If you have been unable to accept the intense emotions evoked by the death, you may experience complicated grief. Or perhaps your family and friends have failed to validate your feelings of loss. Other significant losses occurring at the same time, the inability to participate in the grief process due to personal illness, or the lack of access to the usual rituals, such as a funeral, also may provide the impetus for complicated grief.

Use of drugs or alcohol. Drugs or alcohol may suppress your feelings connected with the loss, thus short-circuiting what may otherwise be a normal and healthy grief journey.

EXPRESS YOURSELF. Go to *The Understanding Your Grief Journal* on p. 123.

Signs of Complicated Grief

When good grief goes bad, a few common behavior patterns emerge. The following patterns sometimes signal the presence of complicated grief:

Postponing your grief. You may find yourself delaying the expression of your grief or hoping that it will go away. Denial is normal and necessary for a short time, but ongoing denial is harmful.

Displacing your grief. Displacing your grief means taking the expression of your grief away from the loss itself and directing these intense feelings toward other things in your life. For example, you may experience difficulty at work or in relationships with other people. You may feel depressed, bitter, and hateful.

Replacing your grief. If you take the emotions that were invested in the relationship that ended in death and reinvest them prematurely in another relationship, you may be attempting to replace your grief. This replacement pattern does not only occur with other relationships, but in other life activities as well. For example, you may become a workaholic although you have never been one in the past.

Minimizing your grief. If you are aware of your feelings of grief but try to downplay them, you may be experiencing complicated grief. You may try to prove to yourself that the loss in your life doesn't affect you very much. Or you may talk openly about how "well you are doing" and how "your life is back to normal" even though the death has just occurred.

Somaticizing your grief. Somaticizing is the clinical expression that describes the attempt to convert your feelings of grief into physical symptoms. You may become so completely preoccupied with your physical problems that you have little or no energy to relate to other people or do your work of mourning.

In summary, complicated grief is grief that has somehow been pulled off the path and needs to find its way back to it. A sensitive, well-trained counselor can help you do that. And remember—deciding to seek professional help from a counselor or therapist, whether your grief journey is complicated or uncomplicated, is not an admission of failure; it is a positive step in your personal development and an important self-care task.

EXPRESS YOURSELF. Go to *The Understanding Your Grief Journal* on p. 123.

Individual Counseling

How to Find a Good Counselor

Finding a good counselor to help you through the grief process sometimes takes a little doing. A recommendation from someone you trust is probably the best place to start. If he or she had a good counseling experience, and thinks you would work well with this counselor, then you might want to start there. Ultimately, though, only you will be able to determine if a particular counselor can help you.

If a friend's recommendation doesn't work out, try more formal searching methods. The following resources may be helpful:

- A local hospice, which may even have a counselor on staff who may be available to work with you.
- A self-help bereavement group, which usually maintains a list of counselors specializing in grief therapy.
- Your personal physician, who can often refer you to bereavement care specialists.
- An information and referral service, such as a crisis intervention center, that maintains lists of counselors who focus on bereavement work.
- A hospital, family service agency, and/or mental health clinic. All usually maintain a list of referral sources.

EXPRESS YOURSELF. Go to *The Understanding Your Grief Journal* on p. 124.

Finding a Grief Counselor

Depending on the size and mental health resources of your community, you may want to seek out not just a good counselor but a good grief counselor. Someone skilled at marital counseling, for example, may have little or no understanding of grief issues.

Scan your Yellow Pages for counselors citing grief or bereavement as a specialty. Another credential to look for is certification from the Association for Death Education and Counseling (ADEC). (Go to adec.org for more information.)

Finally, ask the following questions during your initial consultation with the counselor:

- What are your credentials and where were you trained?
- Have you had specialized bereavement care training?
- What is your experience with bereaved people?
- What is your counseling approach with a bereaved person?

Deciding if a Counselor Is Right for You

Trust your instincts. You may leave your first counseling session feeling you have "clicked" with your counselor. On the other hand, it may well take you several sessions to form an opinion.

In addition to your gut feeling, the following inventory may help you determine whether or not the counselor you have chosen is meeting your needs. You should meet with your counselor a few times before using this test.

0=never
1=slightly or occasionally
2=moderately or sometimes
3=a great deal or most of the time
4=markedly or all of the time

In the blank next to each question, write the number that most applies.

1. _____ *I feel that this counselor understands me.* Empathetic understanding is the basis for the work you will do in a counseling relationship. Does the counselor convey a desire to understand you? Does he listen closely to your thoughts and feelings? If your counselor isn't empathetic, you probably won't feel understood and you will probably not trust this person to help you heal. Be aware, though, that understanding is not the same as total agreement. Sometimes a counselor may understand, but still disagree.

2. _____ *I have a clear understanding of how this counselor will help me with my grief.* A good counselor can help you understand how the counseling process can help you heal, so ask. Express your own counseling goals and see if the counselor agrees that your expectations are realistic. Keep in mind that it may take several sessions to develop mutually agreeable counseling goals.

3. _____ *The counselor seems genuinely interested and attends to what I say.* In other words, do you feel connected to the

counselor? Is she alert, sensitive, and caring? Or does the counselor seem tired, distracted, or overworked? You deserve and need your counselor's full attention. If you aren't getting focused, genuine attention, look for help elsewhere.

4. _____ *What the counselor says about my grief makes sense to me.* Trust your instincts. Unfortunately, some people become victims of misinformed counselors who lack training in bereavement therapy. If the counselor makes comments that reflect judgment instead of understanding, you may want to consider another counseling resource. "You shouldn't feel that way," "Have you thought about what you have to be thankful for?" and "You just have to accept it and get on with life" are inappropriate, judgmental comments.

5. _____ *This counselor encourages me to "teach" him or her about my grief experience.* You are the expert about your own grief. For the counselor to understand your experience, he must allow you to teach him about your grief journey. One clue? If the counselor is talking more than you are, odds are that he is doing the teaching, not you.

6. _____ *My counselor helps me explore areas I might want to avoid.* A helpful counselor will encourage you to talk, think about, and feel certain feelings—sometimes uncomfortable feelings—you may want to avoid. Effective counselors use a skill called "supportive confrontation" to help you participate in the hard work of mourning.

7. _____ *This counselor seems flexible and open to perspectives other than her own.* Openness to different thoughts and ideas is the mark of a good professional. If your counselor is as an "all-knowing expert" who espouses the only "correct" answers, you would probably be better helped by someone more flexible and open.

8. _____ *My counselor is willing to help me explore other sources of support.* While support groups aren't for everyone, many grieving people find them to be a tremendous help. Your counselor should be willing to help you find additional

healing resources. Ask if he is aware of any groups or books that have helped other clients.

9. _____ *Valuable conversation, not small talk, fills our sessions.* While most counseling sessions begin with some "warm-up" and social exchanges, counseling is not chit-chat. If you end up talking about everything but your grief, something is wrong. Either you, the counselor, or both of you are afraid of encountering the feelings of hurt and loss. A helpful counselor will move from warm-up time to focusing on your healing. If you feel like you have a pleasant social experience with your counselor, but aren't making progress in your grief work, discuss this with her.

10. _____ *This counselor is willing to share his own experiences with death when they seem appropriate.* Distant, unexpressive counselors who never talk about their own life experiences do exist, but effective counseling requires a meaningful interchange. Your counselor should openly respond to your questions about his own experiences with death and grief. While the primary focus should remain your grief, it is certainly appropriate to ask if your counselor has experienced the death of someone loved. This doesn't mean that a counselor must have had numerous death experiences to be helpful to you, just that he should be willing to draw from whatever experiences he has had in answering your questions.

11. _____ *My counselor is interested in talking to people important to me—family, relatives, friends—when it seems it would help the counseling process.* An effective counselor will be interested in how you interact with people around you. If you or your counselor decide to exclude these significant influences, counseling may not be as helpful as it could be.

12. _____ *This counselor seems to practice what she preaches.* The helpful bereavement counselor is one who will allow herself to mourn when a death occurs. She mourns in the same healthy ways she recommends for you. Ask your counselor what she has found helpful.

13. _____ *My counselor understands that the concepts of* *"reconciliation," "accommodation," or "integration" are* *more helpful than "resolution" or "recovery."* A good counselor knows that you are forever changed by the death of someone loved. If the counselor's goal is to help you "get over" or "resolve" your grief, he probably isn't the right counselor for you. Your mutual goal should be to learn to live with your grief while at the same time finding continued meaning in living.

14. _____ *This counselor treats me as an equal and relates to* *me in a positive way.* If you feel comfortable with your counselor, you probably feel that way because he treats you with respect. If, on the other hand, your counselor has an air of superiority and formality, consider finding someone else.

15. _____ *My counselor gives me a sense of hope for healing.* Hope for healing is essential to your ultimate reconciliation of the death. No, you won't ever "get over it," but your counselor should help you feel like you're progressing in your work of mourning.

Understanding Your Score

Add up your score and check the total here:

45-60   This counselor is probably a good choice for you.
30-45   Consider finding a more compatible counselor.
0-30   This counselor probably can't help you. Look for another.

Though this is not a scientific inventory, it may provide you with a sense of whether or not you are working with a counselor who is helpful to you.

EXPRESS YOURSELF. Go to *The Understanding Your Grief* *Journal* on p. 124.

If Your Counselor Recommends Hospitalization

If your counselor, doctor, or another professional recommends you enter an inpatient psychiatric hospital for care, be sure to ask the following questions:

- Why should I be hospitalized?
- Which hospitals are there to choose from?
- Where can I get information on these hospitals?
- How long will I be hospitalized?
- How much does it cost?
- What if decide against hospitalization?

Inpatient mental health care can be very beneficial to bereaved people who need to immerse themselves in intense, around-the-clock grief work to heal. But less restrictive therapy options, such as outpatient counseling and support group work, should always be considered first. Many professionals feel that hospitalization is overused, and the costs can be astronomical. If your counselor recommends hospitalization, always ask questions and consider getting a second opinion.

Cost of Counseling

The cost of counseling is an important consideration. You will probably discover that costs vary from region to region and from counselor to counselor. Fees generally range from $75 to $150 per one-hour session.

Your insurance may cover the costs of outpatient counseling sessions, so be sure to ask. If it does, find out how many sessions are covered. Some insurance policies also designate which types of counselors they will reimburse for mental health care.

Some counselors may charge less than their full fee if you have financial limitations and aren't covered by insurance. Some also operate on a sliding scale fee structure, which means they base their fees on their clients' incomes. Don't be afraid to ask your counselor questions about costs and payment options.

If you must pay for the counseling yourself, think of it as an investment in yourself. While you may have difficulty justifying the expense, what could be more important than your physical, emotional, and spiritual well-being? No, you can't drive, eat or wear the results of counseling. But you should consider rediscovering meaning in your life one of the best investments you'll ever make.

Length of Counseling

Some grieving people only need a few sessions, while others benefit from a longer-term counseling relationship. Discuss this issue openly with your counselor and decide what is best for you.

One helpful way to determine an appropriate length of counseling is called a "time contract." With this method, the counselor and client meet for an initial consultation and agree on a certain number of sessions. Again, that number may vary considerably depending on your unique circumstances. At the conclusion of the pre-established number of sessions, the counselor and client discuss the client's progress and determine if additional sessions would be helpful. If the time contract idea appeals to you, bring it up with your counselor.

Regardless of the length of your counseling, it is doubtful that you will feel you are easily, steadily moving forward in your grief journey. More likely, the ebb and flow of pain and healing will at times make you feel you aren't making steady progress. Be patient

"However long the night, the dawn will break."
African Proverb

with yourself as you continue to remember the person who died, while working to embrace meaning in your life. Feeling like you sometimes take two steps backward for every step forward is a normal part of the healing experience.

Glossary of Counseling Terms

Bereavement—physical, emotional, cognitive, social, and spiritual state caused by the death of someone loved.

Ed.D.—Doctor of Education, typically with an emphasis in counseling. May or may not have state licensure.

Grief—the internal suffering caused by the death of someone loved.

L.C.S.W.—Licensed Clinical Social Worker. Has state licensure as well as a masters in social work.

L.P.C.—Licensed Professional Counselor. Has state licensure. May or may not have a masters degree.

L.M.F.T.—Licensed Marriage & Family Therapist. Has state licensure. May or may not have a masters degree.

Mourning—the outward expression of grief and bereavement. "Grief gone public."

M.A./M.S.—Masters of Art/Masters of Science. Has bachelors degree, typically in psychology or behavioral science. May or may not have state licensure.

M.Div.—Masters in Divinity. A degree typically granted to clergy. May or may not have state licensure.

M.S.W.—Masters in Social Work. Does not have state licensure.

Ph.D.—Doctor of Philosophy, typically in psychology. May or may not have state licensure.

Psy.D.—Doctor of Psychology. May or may not have state licensure.

Reconciliation—a renewed sense of energy and confidence felt by the bereaved person together with an understanding of how they have been forever changed by the death.

Sliding scale—a fee structure used by some counselors in which fees are based on their clients' incomes.

Support Groups

How to Find a Support Group

You will probably discover, if you haven't already, that you can benefit from connecting with people who also have had a death in their lives. Support groups, where people come together and share the common bond of experience, can be invaluable in helping you heal. In these groups, each person can share his or her unique grief journey in a nonthreatening, safe atmosphere.

Group members are usually very patient with you and your grief and understand your need for support long after the actual death.

"When one tugs at a single thing in nature, he finds it attached to the rest of the world."

John Muir

You might think of grief support groups as places where fellow journeyers gather. Each of you has a story to tell. Your dispatches from the wilderness help affirm the normalcy of each other's experiences. You also help each other build divine momentum toward healing.

To find a support group in your area, call your local hospice, hospital, or funeral home, or call the National Self-Help Clearing House for a local referral.

Remember that a support group may be just one element in your support system. Some people benefit from seeing a counselor as well as joining a support group.

EXPRESS YOURSELF. Go to *The Understanding Your Grief Journal* on p. 126.

How to Know if You've Found a "Healthy" Support Group

Not all support groups will be helpful to you. Sometimes the group dynamic becomes unhealthy for one reason or another. Look for the following signs of a healthy support group.

1. Group members acknowledge that each person's grief is unique. They respect and accept both what members have in common and what is unique to each member.

2. Group members understand that grief is not a disease, but is a normal process without a specific timetable.

3. All group members are made to feel free to talk about their grief. However, if some decide to listen without sharing, their preference is respected.

4. Group members understand the difference between actively listening to what another person is saying and expressing their own grief. They make every effort not to interrupt when someone else is speaking.

5. Group members respect others' right to confidentiality. Thoughts, feelings, and experiences shared in the group are not made public.

6. Each group member is allowed equal time to speak; one or two people do not monopolize the group's time.

7. Group members don't give advice to each other unless it is asked for.

8. Group members recognize that thoughts and feelings are neither right, nor wrong. They listen with empathy to the thoughts and feelings of others without trying to change them.

EXPRESS YOURSELF. Go to *The Understanding Your Grief Journal* on p. 126.

A Final Word About Reaching Out for Help

As a professional grief counselor, I have been privileged to have thousands of grieving people reach out to me for help. Among other important lessons, they have taught me that sharing their grief with others is an integral part of the healing process.

I hope this touchstone has helped you understand the importance of reaching out for help when you are grieving. Please don't try to confront your grief alone. You need companions— friends, relatives, counselors, others who have experienced a similar loss—who will walk with you as you make the difficult journey through grief.

Touchstone Nine
Seek Reconciliation, Not Resolution

"Mourning never really ends. Only as time goes on, it erupts less frequently."
Anonymous

How do you ever find your way out of the wilderness of your grief? You don't have to dwell there forever, do you?

The good news is that no, you don't have to dwell there forever. If you follow the trail markers on your journey through the wilderness, you will find your way out. But just as with any significant experience in your life, the wilderness will always live inside you and be a part of who you are.

A number of psychological models describing grief refer to "resolution," "recovery," "reestablishment," or "reorganization" as being the destination of your grief journey. You may have heard—indeed you may believe—that your grief journey's end will come when you resolve, or recover from, your grief.

But you may also be coming to understand one of the fundamental truths of grief: Your journey will never truly end. People do not "get over" grief. My personal and professional experience tells me that a total return to "normalcy" after the death of someone loved is not possible; we are all forever changed by the experience of grief.

Reconciliation is a term I find more appropriate for what occurs as you work to integrate the new reality of moving forward in life without the physical presence of the person who died. With reconciliation comes a renewed sense of energy and confidence, an ability to fully acknowledge the reality of the death and a capacity to become re-involved in the activities of living. There is also an acknowledgment that pain and grief are difficult, yet necessary, parts of life.

> *"Truly, it is in the darkness that one finds the light, so when we are in sorrow then this light is nearest to all of us."*
>
> Meister Eckhart

As the experience of reconciliation unfolds, you will recognize that life is and will continue to be different without the presence of the person who died. Changing the relationship with the person who died from one of presence to one of memory and redirecting one's energy and initiative toward the future often takes longer—and involves more hard work—than most people are aware. We, as human beings, never resolve our grief, but instead become reconciled to it.

We come to reconciliation in our grief journeys when the full reality of the death becomes a part of us. Beyond an intellectual working through of the death, there is also an emotional and spiritual working through. What had been understood at the "head" level is now understood at the "heart" level.

Keep in mind that reconciliation doesn't just happen. You reach it through intentional mourning, by

- talking it out.
- writing it out.
- crying it out.
- thinking it out.
- playing it out.
- painting (or sculpting, etc.) it out.
- dancing it out
- etcetera!

146

To experience reconciliation requires that you *descend*, not *transcend*. You don't get to go around or above your grief. You must go through it. And while you are going through it, you must express it if you are to reconcile yourself to it.

You will find that as you achieve reconciliation, the sharp, ever-present pain of grief will give rise to a renewed sense of meaning and purpose. Your feelings of loss will not completely disappear, yet they will soften, and the intense pangs of grief will become less frequent. Hope for a continued life will emerge as you are able to make commitments to the future, realizing that the person you have given love to and received love from will never be forgotten. The unfolding of this journey is not intended to create a return to an "old normal" but the discovery of a "new normal."

EXPRESS YOURSELF. Go to *The Understanding Your Grief Journal* on p. 130.

To help explore where you are in your movement toward reconciliation, the following signs that suggest healing may be helpful. You don't have to be seeing each of the signs for healing to be taking place. Again, remember that reconciliation is an ongoing process. If you are early in the work of mourning, you may not have found any of these signs yet in your journey. But this list will give you a way to monitor your movement toward healing. You may want to place checkmarks beside those signs you believe you are seeing.

Signs of Reconciliation

As you embrace your grief and do the work of mourning, you can and will be able to demonstrate the majority of the following:

_____ A recognition of the reality and finality of the death.

_____ A return to stable eating and sleeping patterns.

_____ A renewed sense of release from the person who has died. You will have thoughts about the person, but you will not be preoccupied by these thoughts.

_____ The capacity to enjoy experiences in life that are normally enjoyable.

_____ The establishment of new and healthy relationships.

_____ The capacity to live a full life without feelings of guilt or lack of self-respect.

_____ The drive to organize and plan one's life toward the future.

_____ The serenity to become comfortable with the way things are rather than attempting to make things as they were.

_____ The versatility to welcome more change in your life.

_____ The awareness that you have allowed yourself to fully grieve, and you have survived.

_____ The awareness that you do not "get over" your grief; instead, you have a new reality, meaning, and purpose in your life.

_____ The acquaintance of new parts of yourself that you have discovered in your grief journey.

_____ The adjustment to new role changes that have resulted from the loss of the relationship.

_____ The acknowledgment that the pain of loss is an inherent part of life resulting from the ability to give and receive love.

Reconciliation emerges much in the way grass grows. Usually we don't check our lawns daily to see if the grass is growing, but it does grow and soon we come to realize it's time to mow the grass again. Likewise, we don't look at ourselves each day as mourners to see how we are healing. Yet we do come to realize, over the course of months and years, that we have come a long way. We have taken some important steps toward reconciliation.

"What wound did ever heal but by degrees?"

William Shakespeare

Usually there is not one great moment of "arrival," but subtle changes and small advancements. It's helpful to have gratitude for even very small steps forward. If you are beginning to taste your food again, be thankful. If you mustered the energy to meet your friend for lunch, be grateful. If you finally got a good night's sleep, rejoice.

One of my greatest teachers, C. S. Lewis, wrote in *A Grief Observed* about his grief symptoms as they eased in his journey to reconciliation:

> *There was no sudden, striking, and emotional transition. Like the warming of a room or the coming of daylight, when you first notice them they have already been going on for some time.*

Of course, you will take some steps backward from time to time, but that is to be expected. Keep believing in yourself. Set your intention to reconcile your grief and have hope that you can and will come to live and love again.

Self-Care Guidelines

Movement toward your healing can be very draining and exhausting. As difficult as it might be, seek out people who give you hope for your healing. Permitting yourself to have hope is central to achieving reconciliation.

Realistically, even though you have hope for your healing, you should not expect it to happen overnight. Many grieving people think that it should and, as a result, experience a loss of self-confidence and self-esteem that leaves them questioning their capacity to heal. If this is the situation for you, keep in mind that you are not alone.

"Everything is gestation and then bringing forth."
Rainer Maria Rilke

You may find that a helpful procedure is to take inventory of your own timetable expectations for reconciliation. Ask yourself questions like, "Am I expecting myself to heal more quickly than is humanly possible? Have I mistakenly given myself a specific deadline for when I should be "over" my grief?" Recognize that you may be hindering your own healing by expecting too much of yourself. Take your healing one day at a time. It will ultimately allow you to move toward and rediscover continued meaning in your life.

One valuable way to embrace your healing is to use the journal that accompanies this book. Write your many thoughts and feelings and you will be amazed at how it helps you embrace your grief. Having your experiences to reflect on in writing can also help you see the changes that are taking place in you as you do the work of mourning.

You can't control death or ignore your human need to mourn when it impacts your life. You do have, however, the choice to help yourself heal. Embracing the pain of your grief is probably one of the hardest jobs you will ever do. As you do this work, surround yourself with compassionate, loving people who are willing to "walk with" you.

EXPRESS YOURSELF. Go to *The Understanding Your Grief Journal* on p. 130.

Hope for Your Healing

The hope that comes from the journey through grief is life. The most important word in the previous sentence is *through*. As you do the work of mourning, you do not remain where you are.

I think about the man I was honored to companion following the tragic death of his seven-year-old son, Adam, in a car accident. He was heartbroken. His soul was darkened. He had to come to know the deepest despair. Yet, he discovered that if he were to ever live again, he would have to work *through* his grief. So, he adopted the mantra, "Work on!"

"Hope is the feeling you have that the feeling you have isn't permanent."

Jean Kerr

150

In his process of conscious intention-setting, he decided to believe that even the most heart-wrenching loss can be survived. Perhaps refusing to give in to despair is the greatest act of hope and faith.

Yes, you go to the wilderness, you cry out in the depths of your despair. Darkness may seem to surround you. But rising up within you is the profound awareness that the pain of the grief is a sign of having given and received love. And where the capacity to love and be loved has been before, it can be again. Choose life!

> *"You don't heal from the loss of a loved one because time passes, you heal because of what you do with the time."*
>
> Carol Crandell

Living in the present moment of your grief while having hope for a good that is yet to come are not mutually exclusive. Actually, hoping and even anticipating can deepen your experience of the moment, and motivate you to "work on!"

Hope and Faith as Trust

In the Introduction to this book, I defined hope as "an expectation of a good that is yet to be." So, living with hope in the midst of your grief is living with anticipation that you can and will go on to discover a continued life that has meaning and purpose. If you are in any way like me, you may sometimes lose hope and need to fall back on your faith.

Sometimes in my own grief journey, when hope seems absent, I open my heart—my well of reception—and find that it is faith that sustains me. Faith that is inspired by the moments when I'm able to find what is good, what is sweet, what is tender in life, despite the deep, overwhelming wounds of my grief. It is the courage of the human spirit that chooses to live until we die that gives me faith. Life will continue and it will

> *"To believe in something not yet proved and to underwrite it with our lives; it is the only way we can leave the future open."*
>
> Lillian Smith

bring me back to hope. If you lose hope along your journey, I invite you to join me in falling back on faith.

Reflect on this: Living with hope is living in anticipation of what can be. Sometimes when you are in the wilderness of your grief, it's easy to question your hope for the future. But living with faith is embracing what cannot be changed by our will, and knowing that life in all of its fullness is still good. Choose life!

Hope and Faith in God

In the religious traditions of Christianity and Judaism, hope is much more than "an expectation of a good that is yet to be."

> *"Every tomorrow has two handles. We can take hold of it with the handle of anxiety or the handle of faith."*
>
> Henry Ward Beecher

Hope is confidence that God will be with you in your grief and, most important, that life continues after death. Hope is trust in God even when everything seems hopeless. Hope is the assurance that God has the last word, and that that word is LIFE—even as you confront the realities of the death of someone you have loved. Choose life!

EXPRESS YOURSELF. Go to *The Understanding Your Grief Journal* on p. 131.

A Final Word About Reconciliation

The word "reconcile" comes from the Middle English for "to make good again." This is the essence of reconciliation in grief, actually—to make your life good again. You have the power to accomplish this. Through setting your intention to heal and intentional mourning, as well as reaching out for help from others, you can and will make your life good again.

In fact, in some ways, your life might be more than good—it might be richer and more deeply-lived. This transformative power of grief is the subject of the tenth and final touchstone.

Touchstone Ten

Appreciate Your Transformation

"Nature does not know extinction, all it knows is transformation."
Wernher Von Braun

The journey through grief is life-changing. When you leave the wilderness of your grief, you are simply not the same person as you were when you entered the wilderness. You have been through so much. How could you be the same?

I'm certain you have discovered that you have been transformed by your journey into grief. Transformation literally means an entire change in form. Many mourners have said to me, "I have grown from this experience. I am a different person." You are indeed different now. Your inner form has changed. You have likely grown in your wisdom, in your understanding, in your compassion.

Now, don't take me the wrong way. Believe me, I understand that the growth resulted from something you would have preferred to avoid. Though grief can indeed transform into growth, neither you nor I would seek out the pain of loss in an effort to experience this growth. While I have come to believe that our greatest gifts often come from our wounds, these are not wounds we masochistically go looking for. When others offer untimely comments like, "You'll grow from this," your right to be hurt, angry, or deeply sad is taken away from you. It's as if these people are saying that you should be grateful for the death! Of course you're not grateful for the death (though you may feel relieved if the death followed a long period of suffering). You would rather the person were still alive and well.

But the person isn't alive and well. He or she has died, you are grieving and, I hope, mourning, and you are probably finding yourself a changed and possibly better person. To understand how transformation in your grief occurs, let us explore some aspects of growth in grief.

EXPRESS YOURSELF. Go to *The Understanding Your Grief Journal* on p. 136.

Growth means change.

We as human beings are forever changed by the death of someone in our lives. You may discover that you have developed new attitudes. You may be more patient or more sensitive to the feelings and circumstances of others, especially those suffering from loss. You may have new insights that guide the way you live your new life. You may have developed new skills. You may have learned to balance your own checkbook or cook a nice meal.

> *"The need for change bulldozed a road down the center of my mind."*
> Maya Angelou

You are "new," different than you were prior to the death. To the extent that you are different, you can say you have grown. Yes, growth means change.

EXPRESS YOURSELF. Go to *The Understanding Your Grief Journal* on p. 136.

Growth means a new inner balance with no end points.

While you may do your work of mourning in ways that help you recapture some sense of inner balance, it is a new inner balance. The word growth reflects that you do not reach some final end point in your grief journey.

Not any one of us totally completes the mourning process. People who think you "get over" grief are often striving to pull it together while at the same time feeling that something is missing.

You don't return to a previous "inner balance" or "normal" but instead eventually achieve a new inner balance and a new normal. Yes, growth means a new inner balance.

EXPRESS YOURSELF. Go to *The Understanding Your Grief Journal* on p. 136.

Growth means exploring your assumptions about life.

The death of someone in your life invites you to look at your assumptions about life. Your loss experiences have a tendency to transform your assumptions, values, and priorities. What you may have thought of as being important—your nice house, your new car—may not matter any longer. The job or sport or financial goal that used to drive you may now seem trivial.

"Loss provides an opportunity to take inventory of our lives, to reconsider priorities, and to determine new directions."
Gerald L. Sittser

You may ask yourself, "Why did I waste my time on these things?" You may go through a re-thinking or a transformation of your previously-held values. You may value material goods and status less. You may now more strongly value relationships.

When someone loved dies, you may also find yourself questioning your religious and spiritual values. You might ask questions like, "How did God let this happen?" or "Why did this happen to our family?" or "Why should I get my feet out of bed?"

Exploring these questions is a long and arduous part of the grief journey. But ultimately, exploring our assumptions about life can make these assumptions richer and more life-affirming. Every loss in life calls out for a new search for meaning, including a natural struggle with spiritual concerns, often transforming your vision of your God and your faith life. Yes, growth means exploring your assumptions about life.

> *"Finding meaning begins in questioning. Those who do not search, do not find."*
> Anonymous

EXPRESS YOURSELF. Go to *The Understanding Your Grief Journal* on p. 137.

Growth means utilizing your potential.

The grief journey often challenges you to reconsider the importance of using your potential. In some ways, death loss seems to free the potential within. Questions such as "Who am I? What am I meant to do with my life?" often naturally arise during grief. Answering them inspires a hunt. You may find yourself searching for your very soul.

> *"What you are is God's gift to you. What you do with what you are is your gift to God."*
> George Foster

In part, seeking purpose means living inside the question, "Am I making a living doing the work I love to do?" Beyond that, it means being able to say, "Does my life really matter?" Rather than dragging you down, your grief may ultimately lift you up. Then it becomes up to you to embrace and creatively express your newfound potential.

Until you make peace with your purpose and using your potential, you may not experience contentment in your life. Joy will come to you when you know in your heart that you are using your potential—in your work or in your free time or in your relationships with friends and family.

I believe that grief's call to use your potential is why many mourners go on to help others in grief. You don't have to discover a cure for cancer. You may volunteer to help out with a grief support group or a local hospice. You may reach out to a neighbor who is struggling or devote more time to your children or grandchildren. Remember—we all have gifts and part of our responsibility is to discover what those gifts are and put them to use. Yes, growth means utilizing our potential.

EXPRESS YOURSELF. Go to *The Understanding Your Grief Journal* on p. 137.

Your Responsibility to Live

"Your joy is sorrow unmasked...

The deeper that sorrow carves into your being, the more joy you can contain.

When you are joyous, look deep into your heart and you shall find it is only that which has given you sorrow that is giving you joy.

When you are sorrowful, look again in your heart, and you shall see that in truth you are weeping for that which has been your delight."

Kahlil Gibran

Paradoxically, it is in opening to your broken heart that you open yourself to fully living until you die. You are on this earth for just a short time. You move through new developmental and spiritual stages daily, weekly, yearly.

"Each day comes bearing its own gifts. Untie the ribbons."

Ruth Ann Schabacker

Sorrow is an inseparable dimension of our human experience. We suffer after a loss because we are human. And in our suffering, we are transformed. While it hurts to suffer lost love, the alternative is apathy. Apathy literally means the inability to suffer, and it results in a lifestyle that avoids human relationships to avoid suffering.

Perhaps you have noticed that some people die a long time before they stop breathing. They have no more promises to keep, no more people to love, no more places to go. It is as if the souls of these people have already died. Don't let this happen to you. Choose life!

Yes, you have to do your work of mourning and discover how you are changed. You have to live not only for yourself, but for the precious person in your life who has died—to work on their unfinished work and to realize their unfinished dreams. You can do this only by living.

> "Life is either a daring adventure or nothing. To keep our faces toward change and behave like free spirits in the presence of fate is strength undefeatable."
> Helen Keller

Ask yourself: Am I doing something about the unfinished acts and dreams of the person who died? If you have in any way "set your intention" to live in pessimism and chronic sorrow, you are not *honoring* your grief, you are *dishonoring* the death.

I truly believe that those who have died before live on through us, in our actions and our deeds. When we honor their unfinished contributions to the living world, our dead live on. When we dedicate ourselves to helping others who come to know grief, they live on.

What if the person who died could return to see what you are doing with your life? Would he or she like how you have been transformed? Would he be proud of you? Would she believe that her life and death brought meaning and purpose to your life? Or, would he see you dying before you are dead?

What if he or she could see that you have mourned but also gone on to help others in grief and sorrow? What if he could see that he left his love forever in your heart? What if she could see that you live your life with passion in testimony to her?

No matter how deep your grief or how anguished your soul, bereavement does not free you from your responsibility to live until you die. The gift of life is so precious and fragile. Choose life!

EXPRESS YOURSELF. Go to *The Understanding Your Grief Journal* on p. 138.

Nourishing Your Transformed Soul

Yes, your soul has been transformed by the death of someone loved. Your soul is not a physical entity; it is everything about you that is not physical—your values, your identity, your memories, even your sense of humor. Naturally, grief work impacts your soul! I often say that grief work is soul work.

"I have been trying to make the best of grief and am just beginning to learn to allow it to make the best of me."

Barbara Lazear Ascher

In part, nourishing your grieving soul is a matter of surrendering to the mystery of grief. As I noted in the beginning of this book, real learning comes when we surrender: surrender our need to compare our grief (it's not a competition); surrender our self-critical judgments (we need to be self-compassionate); and surrender our need to completely understand (we never will). My hope is that the contents of this book have nourished your grieving soul.

There are, of course, many ways to nourish your grieving soul. Here are some that work for me. I nourish my soul. . .

- by attending to those things in life that give my life richness and purpose.
- by trying to fulfill my destiny, by developing my soul's potential.
- by striving to "give back" what others have given to me.

159

- by learning to listen to what is going on around and within me to help me decide which direction I need to go.
- by having gratitude for family and friends.
- by observing what is requesting my attention, and giving attention to it.
- by finding passion in ministering to those in grief.
- by going out into nature and having gratitude for the beauty of the universe.
- by praying that I'm living "on purpose" and using my gifts, whether by writing a book, teaching a workshop, or caring for my children.
- by setting aside time to go into "exile" and be by myself in stillness.
- by earning my living doing something I love to do.
- by going through my own struggles and griefs and realizing that it is working through these wounds that helps unite me with others.

How do you nourish your transformed soul? What can you do today and each and every day henceforth to pay homage to your transformation? How do you most authentically live your transformed life? These are the questions of your present and future life. It is in honoring these questions that you appreciate your transformation and live the best life you can.

"In the midst of winter, I found there was within me an invincible summer."

Albert Camus

EXPRESS YOURSELF. Go to *The Understanding Your Grief Journal* on p. 139.

Carrying Your Transformation Forward

Tomorrow is now. It is here. It is waiting for you. You have many choices in living the transformation that grief has brought to your life.

You can choose to visualize your heart opening each and every day. When your heart is open, you are receptive to what life brings you, both happy and sad. By "staying open," you create a gateway to your healing.

When this happens you will know that the long nights of suffering in the wilderness have given

"What a splendid way to move through the world...to bring our blessings to all that we touch."

Jack Kornfield

way to a journey towards the dawn. You will know that new life has come as you celebrate the first rays of a new light and new beginning. Choose life!

As you continue to experience how grief has transformed you, be open to the new directions your life is now taking. You have learned to watch for trail markers in your grief. Now learn to watch for trail markers in your continued living. Listen to the wisdom of your inner voice. Make choices that are congruent with what you have learned on your journey.

Right now, take a moment to close your eyes, open your heart, and remember the smile of the person in your life who has died.

Bless you. I hope we meet one day.

Directory of Organizations and Support Groups

Bereaved Children
The Dougy Center
P.O. Box 86852
Portland, OR 97286
(503) 775-5683
www.dougy.org

For Widowed People:
AARP, Widowed Persons Service
601 E St. NW
Washington, DC 20049
(202) 434-2277 or
(800) 424-3410
www.aarp.org

THEOS (They Help Each Other Spiritually)
322 Blvd. of the Allies #105
Pittsburgh, PA 15222
(412) 471-7799

For Parents Who Have Experienced the Death of a Child:
The Compassionate Friends
P.O. Box 3696
Oak Brook, IL 60522-3696
(603) 990-0010 or
(877) 969-0010
www.compassionatefriends.org

Parents of Murdered Children
100 East Eighth St., Suite B41
Cincinnati, OH 45202
(513) 721-5683 or
(888) 818-POMC
www.pomc.com

American SIDS Institute
2480 Windy Hill Road, Ste. 380
Marietta, GA 30067
(770) 612-1030 or
(800) 232-SIDS
www.sids.org

Sudden Infant Death
Syndrome Alliance
1314 Bedford Ave., Suite 210
Baltimore, MD 21208
(800) 221-SIDS or
(410) 653-8226
www.sidsalliance.org

Candlelighters Childhood
Cancer Foundation
3910 Warner Street
Kennsington, MD 20895
(800) 366-2223
www.candlelighters.org

For Miscarriage, Stillbirth, Ectopic Pregnancy and Early Infant Death:
International Council on Infertility Information Dissemination (INCIID)
P.O. Box 6836
Arlington, VA 22206
(703) 379-9178
www.inciid.org

St. Joseph's Health Center
Share National Office
300 First Capitol Drive
St. Charles, MO 63301-2893
(636) 947-6164 or
(800) 821-6819
www.nationalshareoffice.com

For Homicide:
Mothers Against Drunk
Driving (MADD)
P.O. Box 541688
Dallas, TX 75354-1688
(800) GET-MADD
www.MADD.org

National Organization For
Victim Assistance (NOVA)
1757 Park Road, NW
Washington, DC 20010
(202) 232-6682 or
(800) TRY-NOVA
www.try-nova.org

Safe Horizon
2 Lafayette St.
New York, NY 10007
(212) 577-7700
24 Hour Hotline:
(212) 577-5777
www.safehorizon.org

For Suicide:
American Association
of Suicidology
4201 Connecticut Ave., NW
#408
Washington, DC 20008
(202) 237-2280
www.suicidology.org

The Samaritans
600 Commonwealth Ave.
Boston, MA 02215
(617) 247-0220
www.samaritansofboston.org

For Terminal Illness:
Make Today Count Cancer
Action Inc.
255 Alexander Street
Rochester, NY 14607
(716) 423-9700
www.canceraction.org

For Hospice Care:
National Hospice and Palliative
Care Organization
1700 Diagonal Rd., Suite 300
Arlington, VA 22314
(703) 837-1500
www.nhpco.org
www.hospiceinfo.org

For AIDS:
AIDS Action
1906 Sunderland Place
Washington, DC 20036
(202) 530-8030
www.aidsaction.org

For Support Groups:
National Self-Help
Clearinghouse
Graduate School and
University Center of the City
University of New York
365 5th Avenue, Suite 3300
New York, NY 10016
(212) 817-1822
www.selfhelpweb.org

For Bereavement Care Training
Opportunities:
The Center for Loss and
Life Transition
3735 Broken Bow Road
Fort Collins, CO 80526
(970) 226-6050
www.centerforloss.com

Helpful Grief Magazines:
Bereavement: A Magazine of
Hope and Healing
(888) 604-4673
www.bereavementmag.com

Grief Digest
www.griefdigest.com

Index

A
accept the reality of the death 89-90
age of the person who died 37
alcohol 81-82, 131
anger 42, 55-58, 130
anniversary 30-31, 84-85
anxiety 54-55

B
belongings of the person who died 78-79, 85
bereavement, definition of 22, 101, 140
birthdays 30, 50, 84
blame 58-61
Borrowed Tears 77

C
circumstances of the death 37
cognitive realm 113-116
companioning 5-7
complicated grief 130-132
confusion 51-54
counseling: see individual counseling
courage 5
crisis 129
crying 27, 76-77
cultural background 42

D
denial 50-51
depression 62-66
  clinical depression 63, 64-65
directory of organizations and
support groups 163
disbelief 48-50
disorganization 51-54
displacing grief 131
divine momentum 4, 38, 125, 141
"doing well" with grief 17-18
dosing pain 13
dreams 52-53, 82-83
drugs 81-82, 131

E
eating 45, 53, 106-107
emotional realm 111-112
exercise 107-108
experiences with loss in the past 44-45
explosive emotions 55-59

F
faith 28, 43, 96, 151-152
fear 54-55
friendships 117
funeral 38-39, 92, 104

G
gender 41-42
"getting over" grief 31-32, 145-147
Glossary of counseling terms 140
goals 115
going crazy 51-52, 69-85
grief attacks: see griefbursts
grief counselor, finding 133
grief map 112
griefbursts 33, 75-76, 104

The Understanding Your Grief Journal
Exploring the Ten Essential Touchstones

Writing can be a very effective form of mourning, or expressing your grief outside yourself. And it is through mourning that you heal in grief.

The Understanding Your Grief Journal is a companion workbook to *Understanding Your Grief*. Designed to help mourners explore the many facets of their unique grief through journaling, this compassionate book interfaces with the ten essential touchstones. Throughout, journalers are asked specific questions about their own unique grief journeys as they relate to the touchstones and are provided with writing space for the many questions asked.

Purchased as a set together with *Understanding Your Grief*, this journal is a wonderful mourning tool and safe place for those in grief. It also makes an ideal grief support group workbook.

ISBN 1-879651-39-4 • 112 pages • softcover • $14.95
(plus additional shipping and handling)

ALSO BY ALAN WOLFELT

The Understanding Your Grief Support Group Guide
Starting and Leading a Bereavement Support Group

For bereavement caregivers who want to start and run an effective grief support group for adults, this new *Support Group Guide* discusses the role of support groups for mourners and describes the steps involved (such as deciding on group format, publicizing the group and writing meeting plans) in getting a group started. Responding to problems in the group is also addressed, as is a model for evaluating your group's progress.

This *Guide* includes potential meeting plans that interface with *Understanding Your Grief* and the companion journal as texts for group participants. In addition, information is included on ceremonies you can use to support people in grief on special occasions and holidays. This *Support Group Guide* is a must for all bereavement group leaders.

ISBN 1-879651-40-8 • 112 pages • softcover • $19.95
(plus additional shipping and handling)

ALSO BY ALAN WOLFELT

The Journey Through Grief
Reflections On Healing
Second Edition

This revised, second edition of *The Journey Through Grief* takes Dr. Wolfelt's popular book of reflections and adds space for guided journaling, asking readers thoughtful questions about their unique mourning needs and providing room to write responses.

The Journey Through Grief is organized around the six needs that all mourners must yield to—indeed embrace—if they are to go on to find continued meaning in life and living. Following a short explanation of each mourning need is a series of brief, spiritual passages that, when read slowly and reflectively, help mourners work through their unique thoughts and feelings.

"The reflections in this book encourage you to think, yes, but to think with your heart and soul," writes Dr. Wolfelt. "They invite you to go to that spiritual place inside you and, transcending our mourning-avoiding society and even your own personal inhibitions about grief, enter deeply into the journey."

Now in softcover, this lovely book is more helpful (and affordable) than ever!

ISBN 1-879651-34-3 • 176 pages • softcover • $16.95
(plus additional shipping and handling)

ALSO BY ALAN WOLFELT

Healing Your Grieving Heart
100 Practical Ideas

When someone loved dies, we must express our grief if we are to heal. In other words, we must mourn. But knowing how to mourn doesn't always come naturally.

This book offers 100 practical ideas to help you practice self-compassion. Some of the ideas teach you the principles of grief and mourning. The remainder offer practical, action-oriented tips for embracing your grief. Each also suggests a *carpe diem*, which will help you seize the day by helping you move toward healing today.

ISBN 1-879651-25-4 • 128 pages • softcover • $11.95
(plus additional shipping and handling)

ALSO BY ALAN WOLFELT

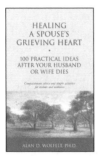

Healing A Spouse's Grieving Heart
100 Practical Ideas After Your Husband or Wife Dies

When your spouse dies, your loss is profound. Not only have you lost the companionship of someone you deeply loved, you have lost the person who shared your history, your helpmate, your lover, perhaps your financial provider. Learning to cope with your grief and find continued meaning in life will be difficult, but you can and you will if you embrace the principles set forth in this practical guide by one of North America's most well-known grief counselors.

Like the other titles in the popular 100 Ideas Series, this book offers 100 practical, here-and-now suggestions for helping widows and widowers mourn well so they can go on to live well and love well again. Whether your spouse died recently or long ago, you will find comfort and healing in this compassionate book.

ISBN 1-879651-37-8 • 128 pages • softcover • $11.95
(plus additional shipping and handling)

ALSO BY ALAN WOLFELT

Healing A Parent's Grieving Heart
100 Practical Ideas After Your Child Dies

The unthinkable has happened: your child has died. How do you go on? What can you do with your pain? Where do you turn?

With a Foreword by bereaved parent and editor of *Grief Digest* Andrea Gambill, this book offers 100 practical ideas that have helped other grieving parents understand and reconcile their grief. Common challenges, such as dealing with marital stress, helping surviving siblings, dealing with hurtful advice from others and exploring feelings of guilt, are also addressed.

ISBN 1-879651-30-0 • 128 pages • softcover • $11.95
(plus additional shipping and handling